OLD WINE
IN A NEW
BOTTLE

STUART LEE

OLD WINE IN A NEW BOTTLE

CLASSIC CARD TRICKS
SPECTACULARLY RE-WORKED

ALL YOU NEED
TO KNOW

Order this book online at www.trafford.com
or email orders@trafford.com

Most Trafford titles are also available at major online book retailers.

Printed in the United States of America.

ISBN: 978-1-4669-4586-9 (sc)
ISBN: 978-1-4669-4587-6 (e)

Library of Congress Control Number: 2012911740

Trafford rev. 07/27/2012

 www.trafford.com

North America & international
toll-free: 1 888 232 4444 (USA & Canada)
phone: 250 383 6864 ♦ fax: 812 355 4082

CONTENTS

INTRODUCTION

THERE ARE SOME CARD TRICKS that can be described as "classic" either because the outcome of the trick is well-known to the audience (for example, where a spectator thinks of a card and the performer then produces or names the thought-of card) or because the trick is of a particular genre (for example, where the location of a card in the pack or deck is discovered by spelling out the name of the card). What this book does is to take a number of these "classic" tricks and, by adapting them, produce a much heightened effect in each case.

The book sets out the complete instructions for the performance of a routine using these tricks. Only a minimum of skill in card manipulation is required to perform the routine and such manipulations as are required are fully explained and described. In addition, complete instructions for the performance of any sleights-of-hand referred to in the text are given – although the routine can be performed without the use of any as the tricks are self-working, the sleights-of-hand being used only to heighten the appearance of the cards being indiscriminately mixed. The basic routine, which can be readily adapted to suit any circumstances, lasts for approximately 25 minutes.

The rest of this introduction is intended for the reader with little or no experience in performing card magic. The more experienced reader may wish merely to cast an eye over it to confirm that there is nothing new to him or her in it. The beginner, however, should not see it as a section that can be skipped over to get to the meat of the book. For him or her it contains information that is essential to a full understanding of later material.

First of all, some definitions:

All 52 cards together are *the pack* or *the deck*

Any part of the pack is *a packet*

A hand (of cards) is a packet that has been dealt to or given to a spectator

To deal consecutively is to deliver to each hand in turn one card until the deal is completed. *To deal the hands individually* is to deliver all the cards required to one hand before proceeding to deal the next hand.

To count cards reversing their order is to place each card as it is counted on top of the previous card. *To count cards without reversing their order* is to place each card as it is counted beneath the previous card.

Face-down and *face-up* cards are self-evident terms, the face of a card being its value and suit.

The long edge of a card, packet, or pack is *the side.*

The short edge of a card, packet, or pack is *the end.*

Front and *forward* and *outward* are away from you, and *rear* and *backward* and *inward* are towards you.

Left and *right* are from your viewpoint.

With the end of the cards or pack pointing towards the spectators, *the outer end* is the end pointing towards the spectators, and *the inner end* is the end pointing towards you.

With the cards or pack held in the right hand and with the outer end pointing towards the spectators, the outer side is to the right and the inner side is towards the left. Similarly, if the outer side is pointing towards the spectators the outer end is to the right and the inner end is to the left.

With the cards or pack held in the left hand and the outer end pointing towards the spectators the outer side is to the left and the inner side is to the right. Similarly, if the outer side is pointing towards the spectators the outer end is to the left and the inner end is to the right.

The fingers are: *first* (or *index*), *second*, *third* (or *ring*), and *fourth* (or *little*, sometimes referred to as "*the pinky*").

To cut and complete is to take a packet of cards from the top of the pack and to place what was the bottom of the pack on top of it. With the cards in hand the same outcome is achieved by *the undercut*, where the bottom part of the pack is cut away and transferred to the top of the pack.

To cull is to extract a card or cards (either openly or secretly) from the rest of the cards in a pack or packet.

An *out-jogged* or *up-jogged* card or packet is a card or packet positioned in the pack so that the card or packet projects from the pack.

A break is a small gap or opening formed secretly within a packet or pack at either the inner end or at the inner corner of the inner side. The former is held by the tip of the thumb of the hand holding the cards and the latter by the tip of the little finger of the hand holding the cards (and for this reason it is sometimes referred to as "*a pinky break*").

A bridged card is a card that has been subjected to pressure either at the sides or the ends to produce a curve along its length or across its width. A forward curve to the face of a card is a *convex bridge*, and a rearward curve to the face of a card is a *concave bridge*.

Having defined some of the terms used in the main part of the book (others will be explained as they arise) we can now turn our attention to the cards that can be used to perform the tricks.

There are two standard sizes for playing cards. One, the larger of the two sizes, is known as *Poker-size*, the other as *Bridge-size*. An example of the Poker-size is the "*Bicycle Rider Back*" pack produced by the U.S. Playing Card Co. It is obtainable in magic shops and some stationery shops and comes in a variety of coloured backs. Examples of the Bridge-size pack are the "*No 1*" pack by the Waddington Playing Card Co. Ltd. (Winning Moves UK Ltd.) and the "*Standard*" playing cards produced and sold by W.H.Smith. These are widely available in the United Kingdom and come either Red-backed or Blue-backed.

The "*Bicycle Rider Back*" has two indexes on the face of each card, ie. the value and suit of the card are shown at the top left and at the bottom right corners. The Waddington "*No 1*" pack and the W.H.Smith pack are four indexed cards with the value and suit of the cards shown at all four corners of the face of each card. (Waddington also produces a four indexed "*No 1 Poker Deck*".) An advantage of a four indexed pack is that irrespective of whether the face of the pack is fanned or spread from left to right or right to left the indexes of the cards are equally observable. Additionally, some performers find the smaller Bridge-size cards easier to handle. However, most performers prefer to use the "*Bicycle Rider Back*" packs as among the many advantages they give are the variety of colours for the backs, the fact that they can be obtained with blank faces, blank backs, doubled-faced, double-backed, and as a miniature size with red, blue or green backs in a design identical to the full-sized packs. They are also available in a number of specially prepared packs to perform particular tricks and effects.

A fourth range of playing cards merits attention and that is the "*Classic*" design produced by the Austrian company Piatnik. They are Bridge-sized cards available in back designs in red or blue and also in special packs (ie. blank backs, blank faces, etc.).

For completeness it should also be noted that W.H.Smith produce and sell miniature "*Patience*" packs in identical back design and colour to their "*Standard*" packs and also a Poker-size pack – this latter pack being a card with two extra-large indexes on the face of the cards.

A few concluding words of advice for the beginner in card magic:

Study the descriptions of the handling and presentation carefully before you attempt to perform them.

Go through the manipulations and presentation slowly on the first attempts.

Try not to look at your hands when shuffling or performing a manipulation.

Perform the manipulations and presentations over and over again in practice and only perform a trick for others when you are totally confident of your ability to do so successfully.

If necessary, distract the attention of the spectators away from the cards by diverting their attention elsewhere. This can be done by talking to them directly and requiring a response or by giving them something to do or to look at.

Do not be afraid when the occasion requires it to perform some manipulations openly. It is surprising what can go unnoticed provided it is done boldly and the attention of the spectators distracted by directing it elsewhere.

When you are performing a trick do not rush the presentation. You know the trick and the effect you are attempting, but, hopefully, it is the first time the spectators have seen the trick performed and to rush the presentation would be to confuse them.

As a general rule, never repeat a trick in the same performance. Exceptions are where the same effect or outcome can be achieved by different means or when the mechanics of the trick are such that it is impossible for the spectators to determine how the effect is brought about.

And **never ever** reveal how an effect has been achieved.

Preparation

To PERFORM THE ROUTINE you require two packs of cards of identical design but with different coloured backs. For the purposes of description in this book it will be assumed that one pack has Blue-backed cards and that the other pack is Red-backed – but any two colours are suitable.

The routine has as its foundation two tricks where the cards in the pack have been arranged (or "*stacked*") before the performance to produce particular outcomes. In addition, if you choose to use a bridged card to control the cutting of the pack you must produce such a card for each of the packs. (*A definition of what is meant by a "bridged card" is given in the previous chapter.*) You should note, however, that the tricks can be performed without the use of such a card and details of how this is done are given with the instructions for the individual tricks in the relevant chapters.

If you do choose to produce bridged cards for each of the packs they should be given a **convex** bridge along their length, ie. the pressure to produce the bridge should be applied to the sides of the cards. Any of the 52 cards in the pack may be bridged, but preferably the card should be easily recognised and remembered by the performer. A suitable card for a Blue-backed pack would be the King of Spades (KS) and for a Red-backed pack a suitable card would be the Queen of Diamonds (QD). Only a very light bridge is required to produce the necessary effect and instructions on how to create such a bridge and how to use the card in the handling of the pack are set out in the relevant section of the chapter on "*Handling and Sleights-of-Hand*".

Having produced the bridged cards you can now move on to the arrangement of the packs for the first two tricks of the routine.

Begin by arranging (or "stacking") the Blue-backed pack or the pack you intend to use for the trick "*Think of a Card – Spell Another*". To do this you require in addition to the 52 cards of the pack four **identical** Joker cards with the same pattern and colour backs and four blank-faced cards with the same backs. The Joker cards in the Waddington "*No 1*" packs (both Bridge-size packs and the Poker-size packs) are identical and as such would require you to obtain only two packs of either size to produce four identical Joker cards. In the other packs the Joker cards differ (being either of a different design or one being "red" and the other "black") so to produce four identical Joker cards you would need to obtain four packs. With regard to the blank-faced cards these can be purchased for the "*Bicycle Rider Back*" pack and for the Piatnik "*Classic*" pack but you will need to make them yourself if you intend to use either the Waddington or the W.H.Smith pack. This can be done using self-adhesive address labels trimmed to size. It might be thought the finish and handling of such doctored cards would attract attention and suspicion but you will see when you come to study the details of the trick in which they are used that this is not so.

Having obtained your four identical Blue-backed Joker cards and your four Blue-backed blank faced cards proceed to arrange the Blue-backed pack:

a. The pack is arranged face-down. (Top) Joker – any
17 cards – Joker – any 8 cards and a bridged card (or
any 8 cards if you are not using a bridged card) – 6C –
10C – AC – 2C – AH – 10H – 2H – JC – JH – JS –
4S – 5H – 8S – QS – QH – 3S – KD – 5D – JD –
9D – 3D – 7D – 8D – QD – any 2 cards (or any 3
cards if you are not using a bridged card).

b. Place the arranged pack in the appropriate carton and
put it aside.

You will have left out of the carton two identical Blue-
backed Joker cards and four Blue-backed blank-faced cards
which you will need later.

You can now turn your attention to pre-arranging (or
"stacking") the Red-backed pack. Before you begin make sure
that you have four Red-backed Joker cards (they do not need
to be identical) and four Red-backed blank-faced cards. Then
begin to pre-arrange the pack as follows:

c. Separate the 52 cards of the pack and order each suit
with the cards face-down as follows:
Hearts/Diamonds:
Top: 3 – 8 – 7 – A – Q – 6 – 4 -2 – J – K – 10 – 9 – 5
Spades/Clubs:
Top: 2 – K – 10 – Q – 7 – 3 – 4 – 9 – 5 – A – 6 – 8 – J

d. Riffle shuffle Hearts into Spades, ensuring that 5H
is the bottom card of the riffled packet. (*For an
explanation of how this is done, see the relevant section
in the chapter "Handling and Sleights-of-Hand".*)

e.   Riffle shuffle Diamonds into Clubs ensuring that JC is the bottom card of the riffled packet.

f.   Place two of the Red-backed Joker cards beneath the 5H and then place the Hearts/Spades riffled packet on top of the other riffled packet.

g.   Place the arranged pack in the appropriate carton and put it aside.

You should now have left two identical Blue-backed Jokers, two Red-backed Jokers, four Blue-backed blank-faced cards and four Red-backed blank-faced cards. Thoroughly mix them and place them between the two cartons of cards.

The two packs are now arranged (or "stacked") ready for the first two tricks of the routine described in the following chapters.

The Routine

PROBABLY THE BEST PIECE of advice that can be given with regard to card magic is to learn and know a small number of tricks thoroughly rather than a great number of tricks superficially. And the next best piece of advice is that the tricks once learned should be used within a set framework. The first piece of advice ensures that the actual performance of the tricks becomes an almost automatic operation, allowing the performer to concentrate his or her attention on the presentation of the effect. The advantages that accrue from the second piece of advice are that any pressure or distraction in having to decide during the performance what comes next is removed and the tricks can be pre-ordered in such a way as to build on each other.

The information set out in this chapter is a basis on which the courses of action recommended above can be achieved. Firstly, it provides a grouping of tricks from which the routine can be derived and the routine can be as short or as long as the circumstances of the performance require. Secondly, it provides a framework that, although pre-ordered, still allows flexibility when that is desirable.

If you examine the general overview of the routine set out on the opposite page, you will see that it has as its foundation two tricks where the cards in the packs have been arranged in a particular order (or "stacked") before the performance to produce a particular effect and that each effect is related to a particular colour indicated by the colour of the back of the pack. In addition there are four other blocks of tricks and you will note that these blocks contain tricks that can be performed with any pack of cards. It is thus possible to begin a routine with either one of the tricks which depend for their effect on the pre-arrangement of the pack and to follow this trick, using the same pack, with a series of tricks which require no pre-arrangement of the pack. In doing so you are lessening the likelihood that the spectators will suspect that the pack was initially stacked, even more so, if, before it was used, it was cut or mixed as explained in the appropriate section of the chapter on *"Handling and Sleights-of-Hand."*

A General Overview

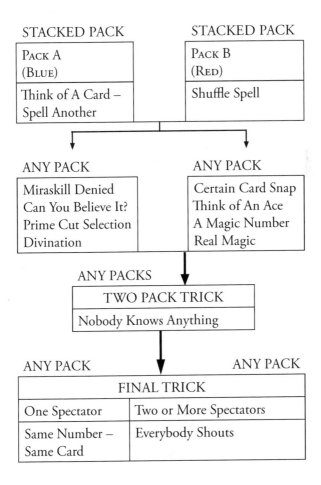

STACKED PACK	STACKED PACK
Pack A (Blue)	Pack B (Red)
Think of A Card – Spell Another	Shuffle Spell

ANY PACK	ANY PACK
Miraskill Denied Can You Believe It? Prime Cut Selection Divination	Certain Card Snap Think of An Ace A Magic Number Real Magic

ANY PACKS

TWO PACK TRICK
Nobody Knows Anything

ANY PACK   ANY PACK

FINAL TRICK	
One Spectator	Two or More Spectators
Same Number – Same Card	Everybody Shouts

This is the basis on which a routine is built and an example will serve to show the flexibility available to suit any circumstances.

The performance begins with the two packs in their cartons on the table and with the mixed packet of Joker cards and blank-faced cards at the side of them.

Given that the spectators do not know what trick is connected with which title or pack (**and they never should**) the routine begins as follows:

"Now, I have some amazing tricks to show you:

The first is ALMOST IMPOSSIBLE.
The second is IMPOSSIBLE.
The third is EVEN MORE IMPOSSIBILE.
The fourth is THE MOST IMPOSSIBLE CARD TRICK IN THE WORLD.
And the fifth is BEYOND THE IMPOSSIBLE.

Now, which one would you like first? (The spectators choose)

And which pack would you like me to do it with? (The spectators choose)

Right – here we go."

You now perform the trick associated with the pre-arranged pack they have chosen and then continue the routine as follows:

"Well, you've had that trick – which one do you want next? (You list the remaining "impossible" tricks and the spectators choose)

And which pack do you want me to use?"

If the spectators choose the pack you have just used for the first trick you go immediately into the first trick of any of the "four-trick any-pack" blocks. If the spectators choose the second pre-arranged pack you perform the trick associated with that pack and then go into the first trick of any of the "four-trick any-pack" blocks.

The situation now is that you have performed two "impossible" tricks – either two pre-arranged tricks or one trick with a pre-arranged pack and one any-pack trick. You then proceed with further any-pack tricks to complete the sequence of five "impossible" tricks. If the spectators have chosen only one of the pre-arranged packs you will have performed all the tricks with that one pre-arranged pack. However, at any point at which the spectators choose the other pre-arranged pack you will perform the trick associated with that pack. In any case, you perform the sequence of five "impossible" tricks.

If you then wish to extend the performance you suggest that you use both packs and proceed to the "two-pack trick" and / or, if you think it appropriate, you may complete the performance with "just one final trick".

All of this then is the framework on which you can build a routine that suits you and the circumstances of the occasion.

Initially, you should concentrate your efforts on mastering the two tricks using the pre-arranged packs and one block of "four-trick any-pack" tricks. Thus you will have at your disposal from the very beginning a routine of up to six tricks based on the two pre-arranged packs (enough for most occasions), and if you are suddenly handed a pack of cards and asked to perform, you have up to four tricks immediately available. This is the firm base on which you can extend to the full repertoire of thirteen tricks.

One final observation: learn and perform the tricks in the "four-trick any-pack" blocks in the order in which they are given. There are two reasons for this. The first is that in doing so you will find them easier to remember and when performing you will be relieved of the pressure of deciding what trick to do next. The second is that they are ordered in such a way that one trick leads naturally into the next and in the case of "*Miraskill Denied*" and "*Can You Believe It*" the first trick sets up the cards to allow you to perform the second trick.

Now, armed with your two packs and with the tricks you have perfected you are ready to produce some magic with cards.

So, on to the tricks.

THE PRE-ARRANGED TRICKS

"Blue Pack" – "Think of A Card – Spell Another"

EFFECT

Cards are dealt randomly to produce four 8-card hands. Each spectator has a free choice of any one of these hands from which they mentally select one card each. Eventually, they spell out their thought-of card from another 8-card packet without revealing the card. When the two cards are revealed they discover they have spelled out each other's card.

PERFORMANCE

1. You begin by asking the spectator to sort out the four Blue-backed blank-faced cards from the eight blank-faced cards and the two Blue-backed Joker cards from the four Joker cards. You take these cards and place them in front of yourself. The Red-backed blank-faced cards and Joker cards you place aside.

2. You now take the Blue-backed carton and take out the cards, taking care not to disturb the order of the cards. Having done so, you perform a false cut followed by a false mix of the pack (*see the relevant sections in the chapter*

on "Handling and Sleights-of-Hand"). If you choose not to perform these moves you merely place the pack face-down on the table.

3. Explain that to perform the trick you require four Joker cards so you will need to extract the two Joker cards from the pack. However, rather than just going through it to find them, you "will try a little magic".

4. Invite a spectator to cut off about the top half of the pack and place it face-down on the table. Point out that as there are two Joker cards in the pack there will be 54 cards in the pack and that half the pack would be 27 cards. Pick up the packet the spectator has placed on the table and count it out face-down into a pile on the table. (*In doing this you are reversing the order of the cards – see the definition of "counting the cards reversing their order" in the "Introduction".*)

5. If on the count you have 27 cards, well and good. If you have more than 27 cards stop the counting at 27 and return the extra cards to the top of the other half of the pack without reversing their order. If you have less than 27 cards in the count make up the number by taking cards off the top of the other half of the pack one at a time and placing them on the face-down pile.

6. Take the cards you have counted out and neaten up the pile. Then instruct the spectator to cut the pile roughly in half and to keep the cards he or she has cut off. You take the bottom part of the pile and place it to one side.

7. Now instruct the spectator **to deal** out the cards he or she
    has into a face-down pile on the table, counting them as
    he or she does so. Take the number arrived at and add the
    two digits of the numbers together to give a single digit
    number (ie. 14 = 1 + 4 = 5). The spectator then takes the
    pile of cards from the table, counts down in the pile to the
    card at that number placing each card face-down in a pile
    on the table. He or she then takes the card at the top of
    the cards of the packet from which he or she is counting
    and places it face-down in front of him- or herself. You
    take the cards that the spectator has left, pick up the pile
    you placed aside at paragraph 6, and place these cards on
    top of the cards you have taken from the spectator. You
    then place this combined packet below the cards that the
    spectator counted off and then place all the cards on top
    of the other "half" of the pack.

8. You now repeat the procedure set out in paragraphs 4-7 to
    find the second Joker. However, this time *you count only
    26 cards.*

9. Turn over the two face-down cards. They are the two Joker
    cards you required. Confirm that as you now have four
    Joker cards you can "get on with the trick".

10. Take the packet you re-constituted at paragraph 8 and
    ask the spectator whether he or she wishes it to be placed
    on top or at the bottom of the cards you put aside at
    paragraph 6. Do as the spectator wishes, pointing out
    that this now gives you a complete pack of 52 cards. Place
    the pack face-down in front of yourself on the table. (*If
    you are using a bridged card to control the cutting of the
    cards you should note that this card was the top card of the*

cards you put aside at paragraph 6. If you are not using a bridged card you should glimpse and remember the identity of the card which is at the bottom of the reconstituted packet from paragraph 7.)

11. You now take the four Joker cards and place them face-down on the table as the bottom cards of what will be four separate face-down piles.

12. Now turn the pack face-up and spread it to show the mix of the cards. Having done so, you turn it face down and cut and complete (*for a definition of "cut and complete" see the "Introduction"*). You then invite the spectators to cut and complete, at will. Finally, you cut the bridged card to the bottom of the pack or if you are not using a bridged pack you turn the pack face-up and spread it to show the mix of the cards – as you do so you split the pack to take the card you noticed at paragraph 10 to what will be the bottom of the face-down pack – you then turn the pack face-down.

13. You begin to deal out the pack placing a card face-down in turn onto each of the face-down Joker cards taking instructions from the spectators as to the order in which the cards are placed. In other words, you will deal out 24 cards – one in turn onto each Joker card, the order of dealing in each four-card group being determined by the spectators. You continue until you have dealt out six cards onto each Joker card. As you deal each card you show it to the spectators telling them that eventually they are going to have to note and remember one of them. (*You do not look at the cards yourself – unless there is only one spectator in which case you are acting in place of a second spectator.*)

14. When the deal is completed place a blank-faced card face-down – one on each pile of face-down cards.

15. You now invite the spectator or the spectators to decide which piles will be paired. (*The trick will work for any two hands.*)

16. When this has been done you pick up each pile in turn and deal them out face-down onto the table, showing each card in turn to the spectator whose pile it is. This, you tell him or her, is to allow him or her to see the cards again and this time to select one mentally and to remember it. You point out that they may, if they wish, select the "*Joker Card*" or "*The Invisible Card*" (ie. the blank-faced card). (*In doing this you are, in fact, reversing the order of the cards into the order required to perform the trick. You place the cards face-down in each pile not looking at them yourself – unless you are acting as a second spectator. In which case the pile you look at will be Pile B – see paragraph 18.*)

17. The piles are now treated in pairs between the spectators or between you and one spectator. Each pair is handled separately as a pair as described below.

18. Treat each pair as A and B (A left; B right). In picking up the piles place A on B and then place the pair you intend to deal with first (or in the case of only one spectator his or her pile and your pile) on top of the other pair. You then place all these cards face-down on the top or at the bottom of the rest of the pack as instructed by the spectator. (*You should note that if you are using a bridged card then this card is now in place to allow the spectators to cut and complete at will. If you are not using a bridged*

card then the card you noted at paragraph 10 will serve the same purpose.)

19. The spectator or spectators are now invited to cut and complete the pack, at will. Finally, if you are using a bridged card you cut that card to the bottom of the pack. If you are not using a bridged card you spread the cards as described at paragraph 12 and this time split the pack **at the card noted at paragraph 10**.

20. Deal out the cards face-down to produce either two 8-card hands or four 8-card hands as appropriate, ensuring that the spectator receives the first hand dealt if there is only one spectator or the spectators receive A and B as they examined the cards to memorise them (A left; B right). The cards are dealt **consecutively** (*see the "Introduction" for a definition of this term*) A and B for the first two hands and then A and B for the second two hands (*Note: these are A and B as they are dealt from the pack*).

21. Take each packet and show the cards in it to the appropriate spectator dealing them out face-down onto the table. Ask the spectator if they see their card in the packet. You do not look at the face of the card unless you are acting as a second spectator (*Note: the dealing has reversed the order of the cards which is what is required for the mechanism of the trick.*)

22. Proceed as follows depending upon the answers:

    a. Both answer "Yes" or both answer "No"
        Place B on A

b. One answers "Yes" the other "No
   Place A on B

23. Now place the packet (or the two packets in appropriate order) on the top of the pack (which has the bridged card or the card noted at paragraph 10 as its bottom card) and proceed as described at paragraph 19.

24. Now repeat paragraphs 20-23 **TWO** more times.

25. You are now going into the final deal to produce the 8-card hands from which the spectators will spell out their cards. To do this proceed as follows: *Deal* off (face-down) in front of yourself A and B (dealing a card **consecutively** to each hand). Invite the spectator who has been receiving A throughout the trick to choose one of the two hands. If the spectator chooses A give it to him or her and instruct him or her to give it to the other spectator. If the spectator chooses B give that hand to him or her and the other hand (A) to the other spectator. In any case, "Spectator A" gets B and "Spectator B" gets A.

26. Now take each packet in turn and deal it out as described at paragraph 21. Ask the spectators if they see their card (their answers are immaterial). Hand the packets back to them and instruct them, in turn, to spell out (silently) their memorised card and to place the appropriate card (unseen) face-down before themselves on the table. (*If you are acting as the second spectator you should state your card and spell it out first.*) The method of spelling to be used, which you can demonstrate using what is left of the pack, is as follows:

a. The top card of the face-down packet is taken to the bottom of the packet as the first letter, the second card is taken to the bottom of the packet as the second letter . . . and so on.

b. The spelling is "A – C – E – O – F – C – L – U – B – S", "N – I – N – E – O – F – H – E – A – R – T – S", etc.

c. The card to be taken is the card arrived at on the final "S" of the suit.

d. However, *you must stress*
    "J – O – K – E – R – C – A – R – D"
        and
    "T – H – E – I – N – V – I – S – I – B – L – E – C – A – R – D"
and the card to be taken is at the final "D" of "C – A – R – D".

If you are in any doubt about the spectator's ability to complete this successfully then have them state their cards and guide them through it.

27. When the spelling is complete ask the spectators what card they were thinking of. When the cards are turned over they will find that in each pair they have arrived at the other's card. (If you are acting as a second spectator you will have arrived at the spectator's card and the spectator will have arrived at your card.)

"Red Pack" – "Shuffle Spell"

EFFECT

The pack is cut and shuffled after which a spectator is asked to choose any suit. This suit is extracted from the pack. The spectator is then asked to choose either of the suits of the opposite colour and this suit is extracted from the pack. These two suits are now shuffled together and the spectator is asked which suit he or she wishes to have. The appropriate suit is then dealt to him or her and the other suit is dealt out to the performer. It is obvious to the spectator that the two packets are in totally different random orders. A spelling out then proceeds whereby one packet spells out the cards as they are turned over from the other packet. Finally, the performer, using a suit chosen by the spectator, spells out any card in that suit thought of by the spectator.

PERFORMANCE

1. Pick up the Red-backed carton and take out the cards, taking care not to disturb the order of the cards. Having done so you perform a false cut of the pack (*see the relevant section in the chapter on "Handling and Sleights-of-Hand"*). If you choose not to perform this move you merely place the pack face-down on the table.

2. Explain that you will need to extract the Joker cards from the pack. (*NOTE: They are in the middle of the pack.*) To do this turn the pack face-up and spread it out until the Joker cards appear. Take them out and place them aside. In doing this keep the two packets that were divided by the Joker cards separate. You now turn over the two

packets and riffle shuffle them into each other. (*For details of how to perform a riffle shuffle see the relevant section in the chapter on "Handling and Sleights-of-Hand"*). In performing the spread and the extraction of the Joker cards you should perform the move quickly as, although the cards are mixed in value and colour, a slow spread might allow a keen-eyed spectator to observe that only two suits are present in each of the packets.

3.   Having riffle shuffled the packets together invite the spectator to choose any suit. Once he or she has done so turn the pack face-up and go through the pack extracting the cards of this suit which should be placed in a face-up pile on the table. The other cards are also placed in a face-up pile on the table. In doing this do not disturb the order of the cards, ie. place the cards one on top of the other as they come out of the pack.

4.   You now ask the spectator to choose a suit of the opposite colour. When he or she has done so pick up the other cards and repeat the procedure of extraction of the suit as described at paragraph 3. You then turn face-down the pile of cards of the non-selected suits and place them to one side.

5.   Take the two piles of face-up cards, turn them face-down and riffle shuffle them into each other.

6.   You now invite the spectators to say which colour suit he or she wishes to have. When he or she has done so, turn the packet face-up and deal out the cards into two face-up piles – the selected suit to the spectator and the other suit to yourself. In doing so do not disturb the order of the

cards, ie. place them one on top of the other as they come out of the face-up packet.

7. In order for you to now bring the trick to its conclusion, you must know how it is structured. You have on the table two piles of face-up cards – one of a red suit and the other of a black suit. You should note that the black suit, using the spelling-out system to be described later, will spell out the cards of the red suit as they are turned over but you should also note that this will only be achieved if the top card of the red pile when that pile is turned face-down is the 3, and when the top card of the black pile when that pile is turned face down is the 2. What you must now do therefore is to arrange the cards in this way. This is done on the subterfuge of establishing that both you and the spectator have all the thirteen cards of the appropriate suit. You do this by counting each pile in turn. If the cards of the pile are correctly configured you count the pile without reversing the order of the cards (*see the relevant section in the "Introduction"*). If the cards of the pile are **not** correctly configured you count the cards reversing their order. Having done this you place each pile face down on the table – the appropriate pile in front of the spectator and the other pile in front of yourself.

8. If the spectator has the red suit instruct him or her to turn over the first card on the top of the pile in front of him or her and to place it face-up on the table by the side of the pile (*NOTE: It should be the 3*). You then pick up your pile and spell out the value of the card ("T-H-R-E-E") and for each letter you transfer a card face-down (unseen) from the top to the bottom of your packet. You then take the top card of the packet, turn it over and place it face-up in

front of yourself. It will be the 3. You go through the piles repeating this process. In each case you will spell out the card turned over by the spectator and you will each finish with a pile of face-up cards in front of you.

9. If at paragraph 8 **you** have the red suit turn over the first card on the top of your pile and place it face-up on the table by the side of your pile. (*NOTE: It should be the 3*). You then instruct the spectator to pick up his or her pile and to spell out the value of the card ("T-H-R-E-E") using the spelling system described at paragraph 8. He or she will spell out the card turned over by you and you will each finish with a pile of face-up cards in front of you.

10. You may if you wish finish the trick at this point but, if you choose to do so, you may extend it as follows:

    a. The two face-up piles on the table are so configured that if you pick up any one of them, turn it face down, and spell out the cards from Ace to King in that order using the spelling system described at paragraph 8 you will spell out the suit in sequence.

    b. You may therefore now invite the spectator to think of any card in either of the suits. When her or she has done so pick up the two piles and, after turning them face down, riffle shuffle them into each other.

    c. You now ask the spectator to declare the suit of the thought-of card.

    d. When the spectator has done so you pick up the face-down riffled packet and, with the faces of the cards towards you and the back of the cards towards the spectator, you go through the packet placing the cards of the declared suit face-up in a pile on the table and the cards of the other suit (without showing them) face-down in a pile on the table in the order in which they came out of the packet.

e. Now on the subterfuge of confirming that you have all thirteen cards of the suit you count them reversing their order and then turn the packet face-down.

f. You take the face-down packet and begin to spell out the cards from Ace through to King, using the spelling-out procedure described at paragraph 8. At each appropriate card you take the card from the top of the pack, without revealing it, and place it face-down, forming a face-down pile on the table. Instruct the spectator to inform you when you have spelled out the value of the thought-of card. When he or she does so and when you turn the card at the top of the face-down pile over it will be the spectator's thought-of card.

THE ANY-PACK TRICKS

"Miraskill Denied"

EFFECT

The pack is thoroughly shuffled. The performer then demonstrates that if a pack is dealt out in pairs there is an almost certain probability that there will be a number of like pairs (ie. Red/Red and Black/Black) in the dealing and that the number of Red pairs will equal the number of Black pairs. The performer does this with fewer and fewer cards until from a very small packet the performer produces one red pair and one black pair. He or she then takes the whole pack, shuffles it, shows the mix of the pack, and states that he or she will perform the almost impossible feat of dealing out the whole pack without producing a single like pair. This the performer then proceeds to do.

PERFORMANCE

1. By way of introducing the trick inform the spectators that a classic trick developed by a card magician in the 1930s (Stewart James) was given the name *"Miraskill"* and is based on the observation that if you take a pack of cards, shuffle it, and deal it out in pairs of cards, there is an almost certain probability that you will produce an equal number of red and black pairs.

2. Proceed to demonstrate that this is so by shuffling the pack, allowing the spectator to shuffle the pack, and by then inviting the spectator to deal out the pack in pairs of cards. (*NOTE: Your shuffle should be a riffle shuffle – see the relevant section in the chapter on "Handling and Sleights-of-Hand" for how to perform a riffle shuffle. The spectator may shuffle or mix the cards as he or she wishes.*)

3. The spectator should take the face-down pack and turn over the cards in pairs from the top of the pack. The like pairs should be placed face-up on the table – the Red/Red in one pile and the Black/Black in a second pile. Any unlike pairs should be handed to you. As you take these cards separate them one to each hand ostensibly to show off a red card and a black card. However, as you bring them together ensure that you order them so that when you turn them face-down and place them on a discard pile the red card will be the top card of the pair. Do this quickly while encouraging the spectator in his or her dealing out of the pairs. (*NOTE: What you are doing is to make up a face-down discard pile which consists of unlike pairs in the sequence Red/Black Red/Black etc throughout the pile.*)

4. When the dealing out is completed invite the spectator to confirm that he or she has an equal number of black and red pairs. (*NOTE: In the very unlikely event that no pairs have been produced (**which is very, very unlikely**) express your surprise, and suggest that the spectator takes out a subscription to the National Lottery, and repeat paragraphs 2-4.*)

5. Invite the spectator to shuffle together or thoroughly mix the cards he or she has counted out. Take the shuffled packet, turn it face-up, and spread it to show the mix. In

splitting it into two packets for a riffle shuffle ensure that the bottom card of each packet is of the same colour. Then riffle shuffle the two packets together, ensuring that in the shuffle the bottom cards of each packet drop together. (*NOTE: This* **guarantees** *that there will be at least one red pair and one black pair in the dealing out of the packet.*)

6.   Point out that there are now fewer cards but that the probability of producing like pairs from it is still very high. Hand the packet to the spectator and instruct him or her to repeat the procedure set out at paragraph 3. Again, you deal with the unlike pairs as described in paragraph 3.

7.   Continue the procedure set out at paragraphs 2-6. As the packet reduces to very few cards it is advisable that you not only shuffle the cards but that you also turn over the pairs of cards yourself. Continue the procedure until only one red pair and one black pair is produced. Take these pairs and, in turning them face down to place them on the discard pile, ensure that the red cards slide into the black cards to produce a Red-Black-Red-Black sequence when the cards are placed face-down on the pile.

8.   Now take the discard pile and mix it using a Charlier Shuffle (*see the relevant section in the chapter on "Handling and Sleights-of-Hand" for how to perform this shuffle*). Then allow the spectator to cut and complete the pack, at will (*for a definition of the term "cut and complete" see the "Introduction"*).

9.   You now Charlier Shuffle again and then finally allow the spectator to cut and complete the pack. When the cutting has been completed you pick up the face-down pack and, with the faces of the cards towards yourself and

the back of the cards towards the spectator, you divide the pack into two packets, ensuring that the face cards (ie. the bottom cards of the packets when they are face-down) are of a different colour. You then turn the packets face-down and riffle shuffle one packet into the other.

10. Having done this turn the pack face-up and spread it to show the mix of the cards. While you are doing this you declare that you will now guarantee to do something that is all-nigh impossible, ie. that you will deal out the pack in pairs without producing a single like pair.

11. You proceed to do so handling the cards as described below:

   a. From the face-down packs turn the cards face-up in pairs and rest them on top of the face-down pack.

   b. If the red card is the top face-up card of the pair move that card slightly away from the pack, place the black card on top of it and then place both cards face-down on the table, declaring "a red and a black" as the base of a face-down pile.

   c. If the black card is the top face-up card of the pair push the red card from beneath it away from the pack and slide the black card on top of it before placing both cards face-down on the table, declaring "a black and a red".

12. You will go through the pack producing only unlike pairs. (*NOTE: You are also producing a face-down pack with the cards arranged in such a way as is required for the trick "Can You Believe It?"*)

"Can You Believe It?"

EFFECT

The pack is thoroughly mixed and cut by the performer and the spectators. Each of two spectators is then dealt two face-down cards from which each secretly selects one card. The cards are returned to the pack which is shuffled and cut. The cards are then dealt out into four piles, alternating face-up and face-down, producing a pile of red face-up cards, a pile of black face-up cards, and two piles of face-down cards. Each spectator is handed a pile of face-up cards and a pile of face-down cards and instructed to shuffle them together to produce a face-down packet. Each spectator then deals out their shuffled packet face-up to produce a pile of cards that are all of one colour except for one card which is of the opposite colour. The card of the opposite colour will be their selected card.

PERFORMANCE

(*NOTE: This trick depends for its successful outcome on the use of the pack from the performance of the trick "Miraskill Denied". It does not need to follow that trick immediately but, when it is performed, the order of the cards from the conclusion of "Miraskill Denied" must not have been disturbed.*)

1. Take the pack in the order it was left at the conclusion of the trick "*Miraskill Denied*" and give it a Charlier Shuffle or mix (*see the relevant section in the chapter on "Handling and Sleights-of-Hand" for how to perform this shuffle*). Then allow the spectators to cut and complete

the pack, at will (*for a definition of the term "cut and complete" see the "Introduction"*).

2. You now Charlier Shuffle again and then finally allow the spectators to cut and complete the pack, at will. When the cutting has been completed you pick up the face-down pack and, with the faces of the cards towards yourself and the backs of the cards towards the spectators, you note the colour of the bottom card of the pack.

3. Now deal off the top of the **face-down** pack two cards **face-down** to each spectator. Deal out the cards as indicated below:

Spectator A		Spectator B	
1	3	2	4

    (If there is only one spectator available you should act as Spectator B.)
    (*NOTE: Spectator A now has two cards of the same colour and the colour is the opposite colour to that of the card at the bottom of the pack. Spectator B (or you if you are acting as the second spectator) also has two cards of the same colour – in this case the same colour as that of the card at the bottom of the pack.*)

4. Instruct each spectator to choose either one of the two cards they have and to take it and note it secretly. (If you are acting as the second spectator you should note one of your two cards). While this is being done you should return the two cards not chosen to the top of the pack in the order of Spectator B's card first and Spectator A's card

second, ie. Spectator A's card is the top card of the face-down pack.

5. You now invite Spectator B to place his or her noted card face-down on top of the pack – and then likewise Spectator A.

6. Immediately, cut the pack into two roughly equal packets, ensuring that on splitting the pack the two packets have different coloured bottom cards. You now riffle shuffle the two packets together, this time ensuring that the top two cards of the pack remain as the top two cards of the riffled pack. (*For details of how this is done, see the relevant section in the chapter on "Handling and Sleights-of-Hand"*).

7. Now deal out two cards face-down from the top of the face-down pack. They should be dealt thus:
   Position 1   Position 2
   (*NOTE: The card at Position 1 is Spectator A's chosen card of which you know the colour and the card at Position 2 is Spectator B's chosen card which is of the opposite colour.*)

8. You continue dealing out from the top of the face-down pack in a procedure that appears complicated on first-reading but which you will find extremely straightforward once you have gone through it with the cards. The procedure is as follows:

   a. Turn the next card you take from the top of the pack face-up. If it is the same colour that you know Spectator A's card is, place it at Position 4. If it is the opposite colour to that you know Spectator A's card is place it at Position 3.

Position 1	Position 2
Position 3	Position 4

b. Take the next card from the top of the pack face-down and place it face-down on the face-down card at the diagonal to which you placed the face-up card, ie. if you placed the face-up card at Position 3 the face-down card is placed at Position 2; if you placed the face-up card at Position 4 the face-down card is placed at Position 1.

c. Turn the next card from the top of the pack face-up. You will have a face-up card at either Position 3 or Position 4. If the card you have taken from the top of the pack is the same colour as the face-up card on the table place it face-up on the top of that card. If the card you have taken from the pack is the opposite colour to the face-up card on the table place it face-up at the unoccupied position.

d. Take the next card from the top of the pack face-down and place it face-down on the face-down card at the diagonal to which you placed the face-up card.

e. Continue in this way through the pack placing face-up cards on the appropriately coloured face-up card position and the following face-down card face-down at the diagonal position.

f. The end result is that you now have on the table:
Position 1: Face-down cards (all of one colour) and Spectator A's selected card of a different colour, (also face-down).

Position 2: Face-down cards (all of one colour) and Spectator B's card of a different colour, (also face down).
Position 3: Face-up cards (all of one colour) and different in colour to Spectator A's selected card.
Position 4: Face-up cards (all of one colour) and different in colour to Spectator B's selected card.

9. Hand the cards at Position 3 to Spectator A and instruct him or her to turn them face-down and shuffle them into the already face-down cards at Position 1.

10. Hand the cards at Position 4 to Spectator B and instruct him or her to do likewise with the cards at Position 2 (or, if you are acting as Spectator B you perform this procedure).

11. Having done this each spectator should turn their packets face-up and either spread out the cards or deal out the cards. They will each find that they have all the cards of the pack of one colour except one which will be of the opposite colour – and the card of the opposite colour will be their selected card. (*NOTE: If you are acting as Spectator B you should allow Spectator A to go first before you declare your selected card and turn over your packet.*)

"Prime Cut Selection"

Effect

A spectator is given a completely free choice of card which he or she secretly notes and returns to the pack. The spectator then cuts a packet from the pack. Using this packet the performer deals a packet of cards from it and invites the spectator to select any number he or she wishes from 1 to the number of cards in the packet. Using that number the performer proceeds to eliminate cards in the packet finishing with one face-down card which proves to be the spectator's selected card.

Performance

1. Allow the spectator to shuffle the pack and to cut it, at will. Take the pack and shuffle it yourself – finally cutting the bridged card to the bottom of the pack. If you choose not to use a bridged card you should glimpse and note the identity of the bottom card of the pack after your shuffle.

2. Invite the spectator to cut off three approximately equal packets from the top of the face-down pack to choose one of the packets, and from that packet to choose any card, which he or she should secretly note.

3. When the spectator has selected his or her card take all the other cards and place them on top of what was the bottom part of the pack, ensuring that either the bridged card or your noted card remains at the bottom of the pack.

4. Now allow the spectator to return the selected card to the pack – on the top, or the bottom, or in the "middle", using the bridged card to bring the selected card to the top of the pack (*for details on how to do this see the relevant section in the chapter on "Handling and Sleights-of-Hand"*). If you are not using a bridged card allow the spectator to replace his or her selected card on either the top or the bottom of the pack and to then cut and complete the pack (*for an explanation of the term "cut and complete" see the "Introduction"*). When the cutting is completed take the pack, holding it so that the faces of the cards are towards you and the backs of the cards are towards the spectator. Split the pack at the point in the pack where you see your noted card and then turn the two packets face-down. One packet will have your noted card as the bottom card, the other will have the selected card as its top card. You may then either place the packet with your noted card beneath the other packet or you may riffle shuffle the two packets into each other, ensuring that the top card of the packet not containing your noted card drops as the top card of the riffled pack (*for details on how to do this see the relevant section of the chapter on "Handling and Sleights-of-Hand*).

5. Place the pack face-down on the table and invite the spectator to cut off a packet of cards from the top of the pack. This packet he or she hands to you.

6. Deal out face-down from the top of the packet seven cards and then pause. Ask the spectator if he or she wishes you to deal any more cards. If the answer is "yes" deal off a further four cards – and pause again. Repeat the question – if the answer is again "yes" deal off a further two cards.

7. You now have seven, eleven, or thirteen cards in a face-down pile on the table. Pick up the packet and count it out without reversing the order of the cards (*see the "Introduction" for details on how to do this*).

8. With the packet face-down ask the spectator to select any number from 1 up to and including the number of cards in the packet. Once the spectator has done so you then proceed to reveal the selected card using the procedure set out below.

    a. Using the spectator's chosen number, say 4, take off in turn cards from the top of the face-down packet and, without revealing them, place them face down at the bottom of the packet. With the 4th card (ie. the final card) turn it face-up and then place it at the bottom of the packet.

    b. Count again 4 cards off the top of the pack as in paragraph a above.

    c. Continue with this process, taking both face-up and face-down cards, until there is only one face-down card left in the packet. This will be the spectator's selected card.

    If the spectator chooses 1 as the number count out "1" and slide the bottom card away from the packet. Turn it face-up and place it on top of the packet. If the spectator chooses the total number of cards in the packet as the number count out that total transferring cards *face-down* to the bottom of the packet and then turn the packet face-up to reveal the card.

"Divination"

EFFECT

The pack is divided into two packets – one packet consisting of the red cards, the other all the black cards. The spectator is invited to choose any one of the packets, the performer takes the other packet. The performer then declares that the trick requires that both the performer and the spectator have an equal number of like pairs. The spectator determines how many pairs each will have and these are sorted out from the packets. After a series of shuffles and cuts the two series of pairs are dealt out – one to the spectator and one to the performer. The packets receive one final cut. The performer then takes a card from the spectator's face-up packet and places it on the table face-up (say, a 6). The spectator now takes any card he or she wishes from their face-up packet and places it face-up on the table (say, a 9). These two numbers are then added together (ie. 6 + 9 = 15). The performer counts out 15 cards from the face-down packet and arrives at a 9, the same value as the card selected by the spectator. The trick can be repeated as many times as the spectator or the performer wishes.

PERFORMANCE

1. Begin by dividing the pack into two packets – one of all the red cards and the other of all the black. Allow the spectator to choose one of the packets.

2. Explain that the trick requires that you each have an equal number of like pairs (e.g. two Aces, two 2s, two 3s, etc) and that he or she can choose how many pairs. Point out, however, that any number from five to thirteen makes for

a more interesting trick. When her or she has chosen the number, say 9 – explain that each of you now needs to extract from your packet the two Aces, two 2s, two 3s, two 4s, two 6s, two 7s, two 8s, and two 9s. If the spectator had chosen above this number you would need to go on to the two 10s, two Jacks (11), two Queens (12) and two Kings (13).

3. Instruct the spectator to extract the appropriate number of pairs from his or her packet. While the spectator is doing this you too extract the appropriate pairs. However, as you do so, you arrange the cards to provide two ascending sequences. For example with the cards at paragraph 2 above your cards would be ordered Ace – 2 – 3 – 4 – 5 – 6 – 7 – 8 – 9 – Ace – 2 – 3 – 4 – 5 – 6 – 7 – 8 – 9 when your packet was turned face down. (The positioning of the suits is immaterial.)

4. Once both you and the spectator have completed the sorting out place the unwanted cards aside and instruct the spectator to give his or her packet a good shuffle and mix.

5. You then take your face-down packet and place it on the table. Allow the spectator to cut and complete as many times as he or she wishes (*for an explanation of this term see the "Introduction"*). You pick up the packet and observe that rather than shuffle it where you will have control of the cards you will allow the spectator to determine how the cards are mixed. You then perform a Charlier Shuffle or mix allowing the spectator to determine how many cards you take at each stage (*for details on how to perform this shuffle see the chapter on "Handling and Sleights-of-Hand"*).

6. When the Charlier Shuffle is completed allow the spectator to cut and complete the packet, at will.

7. As you pick up the packet note the bottom card – this is your key card.

8. You now ask the spectator to take his or her packet and to turn it face up and to shuffle it. You then choose a card from the face-up packet and place it face-up on the table. (*NOTE: The card you choose should be the number of the pairs each of you has **minus** your key card value. For example, if you each have nine pairs and the value of your key card is a 6 the card you choose will be a 3, ie. 9 – 6 = 3. If the value of your key card is a 9 the calculation would be 9 – 9 = 0 and in this case you would not choose a card but you would invite the spectator to choose any card he or she wished and use the value of that card to determine the number of cards you counted down to in your packet – see paragraphs 9–11 below.*)

9. You now invite the spectator to select any card he or she wishes from the face-up pack and place it face-up by the side of the card you have chosen. Add the value of these two cards together (with Jacks = 11, Queens = 12, Kings = 13, if these pairs have been used). Point out that in arriving at this number your card was chosen before the spectator made his or her choice. You may also, if you wish, allow the spectator to change his or her card to arrive at a different number.

10. Once the number has been arrived at replace the card you chose in the face-up packet, leaving the spectator's face-up card on the table.

11. You now count off from the top of your face-down packet cards equal in number to the numbers arrived at in paragraph 9 above, taking each card as you count it to the bottom of the packet (face-down). When you arrive at the card corresponding to the number place it face-down by the side of the spectator's face-up card and instruct the spectator to turn it face-up. It will be of the same numerical value as the spectator's selected card.

12. You may, if you wish, now repeat the trick. If you choose to do so, proceed as follows:

   a. Replace the spectator's card in the face-up packet and replace your own card face-down on top of your face-down packet.

   b. As you now know the value of the top card of your packet it is possible for you to calculate the value of the bottom card of your packet, ie. it is 1 less in value than the top card – if the top card is a 4 then the bottom card is a 3. **This is your new key card.** You should note that if the top card of your packet is an Ace then the bottom card is the value of the total number of pairs in the packet, eg. if the sequences are Ace to King then the bottom card is a King (13).

   c. You now proceed to repeat the procedure described in paragraphs 8–11 above. Alternatively, you may allow the spectator to cut and complete the packet and repeat the trick beginning at paragraph 5 above.

"Certain Card Snap"

EFFECT

A spectator shuffles the pack. The performer instructs him or her to remove any four cards to reduce the pack to 48 cards. The performer shuffles these cards and counts them out face-down onto the table into six 8-card hands. Each of the spectators chooses any hand, mentally selects a card, and shuffles the cards again. The pack is re-constituted, cut by the spectators, and dealt out into eight 6-card face-down hands. The spectators examine the hands and take the hand in which they find their mentally selected card. When their hands are combined and dealt out the spectators are asked to play a form of "SNAP" in which each turns over the other's card.

PERFORMANCE

1. This trick is best performed with two spectators. However, if a second spectator is not available you may take that part.

2. Begin by inviting one of the spectators to shuffle the pack and to extract any four cards from within it to produce a 48-card pack. Place the four extracted cards aside.

3. You take the pack and shuffle it and then cut the bridged card to the bottom of the pack. If you are not using a bridged card you merely shuffle the pack.

4. You now take the pack and count out without reversing the order of the cards six 8-card face-down hands, counting out each hand in turn (*see the "Introduction" for*

an explanation of "counting out without reversing the order of the cards") (NOTE: If you are using a bridged card this procedure ensures that the bridged card is at the bottom of the last hand counted out. You should note and remember the position of this hand.)

5. You now instruct the first spectator (Spectator A) to take any one of these hands to shuffle it, and mentally select any of the cards in the hand. He or she then shuffles the hand again and places it face-down on the table. From the five remaining hands Spectator B does the same.

6. For each of the spectators you take two of the non-selected hands and invite the spectator to place his or her hand between them. (*NOTE: If neither of the spectators has chosen the hand with the bridged card at the bottom ensure that this hand with the bridged card at the bottom is placed beneath the hand of Spectator A. If the hand with the bridged card has been chosen or if you are not using a bridged card note the card at the bottom of the hand that is placed beneath Spectator A's hand.*)

7. Now take the cards within which Spectator B has placed his or her cards and put these cards on top of the cards within which Spectator A has placed his or her cards. The spectators may then cut and complete at will (*see the "Introduction" for an explanation of "cut and complete"*). Finally, you cut either the bridged card to the bottom of the pack or, after turning the cards face-up and spreading them to show the mix, you cut the pack to place your noted card at the bottom of the face-down pack. You then deal out from this pack eight 6-card hands, placing a card

in turn on each hand, the order of dealing in each 8-card dealing sequence being determined by the spectators.

8. You now pick up each hand in turn and, with the backs of the cards towards yourself, you fan or spread the cards and ask each spectator to say if they see their card.

9. If neither does discard the hand. When Spectator A does take that hand and place it face-down in front of yourself and to the left. When Spectator B does take that hand and place it face-down in front of yourself and to the right.

10. Now place Spectator A's cards on top of Spectator B's cards. As you are picking up the cards and going through this move explain to the spectators they are now going to play a game of "SNAP".

11. Deal out face-down cards from the packet to the spectators. Deal the cards to each spectator *consecutively* beginning with Spectator A (*For an explanation of the term "consecutively" see the "Introduction".*)

12. Remind them that when they see their card they should say "SNAP!"

13. Invite Spectator B to turn his packet of cards face-up – when he or she does so Spectator A should see his or her card and say "SNAP".

14. Now invite Spectator A to turn over the top card of his packet – when he or she does so Spectator B should see his or her card and say "SNAP".

15. In the event of both spectators seeing their card in the
    same hand take that hand and place it face-down in
    front of yourself on the table. Gather up all the other
    hands and place them aside. Now deal out face-down
    onto the table the cards of the selected hand, dealing:

1	2	3
4	5	6

    (This will place the spectators' cards at positions 2 and 5.
    A's card at position 2 and B's card at position 5.) Group the
    face-down cards in pairs: 1/4, 2/5, 3/6. Tell the spectators
    that you will "take out" a pair – which you do, either 1/4
    or 3/6. Assuming that you have taken 1/4, you place this
    pair face-down in front of yourself on the table. You then
    invite one of the spectators to "take out" a pair. If the
    spectator chooses 3/6 take this from him or her and place
    it face-down in front of yourself, leaving 2/5 face-down
    on the table. If the spectator chooses 2/5 pick up 3/6 and
    place it face-down in front of yourself. In any case, the
    required pair 2/5 is either in the spectator's hands or on
    the table. If the spectator has the cards in hand instruct
    him or her to keep one card and give the other card to the
    other spectator. If the cards are on the table each takes one
    of the cards. Invite them now to turn the cards face-up
    and say "SNAP" if they see their card.

"Think of An Ace"

EFFECT

A spectator is asked to think of one of the four Aces. The Aces are placed in the pack and as each Ace is placed the pack is cut by the spectator. The pack is then dealt out into four hands, one of which is chosen by the spectator. From this hand the spectator spells out the thought-of card.

PERFORMANCE

1. Extract the four Aces from the pack and place them face-up on the table, overlapping each other so that only the left-hand index is displayed in the order AC (bottom), AH, AS, AD (top fully displayed). (*NOTE: A useful mnemonic is "**C**urly **H**air **S**ettles **D**own".*)

2. Shuffle the rest of the pack and cut the bridged card to the bottom of the pack. If you are not using a bridged card proceed to paragraph 10.

3. Instruct the spectator to look at the Aces and to think of and remember any one of them.

4. Collect the Aces together and turn them face-down (*NOTE: They should now be from the top AC – AH – AS – AD.*)

5. Take each Ace, separately and in turn, off the top of the face-down pile of Aces and place it in the "middle" of the pack under control of the bridge card (*for details on how this is done see the relevant section in the chapter on*

"Handling and Sleights-of-Hand"). Each time an Ace is placed in the pack allow the spectator to cut and complete the pack before the bridged card is cut to the bottom of the pack (*for an explanation of the term "cut and complete" see the "Introduction"*). On the final cut of the bridged card to the bottom of the pack the Aces will be at the top of the face-down pack in order from the top AD – AS – AH – AC.

6. The spectator may now cut and complete the pack, at will. When the cutting has been completed the bridged card should be cut to the bottom of the pack.

7. Now deal out the top 13 cards of the face-down pack into a face-down pile on the table, then the next 13 cards, then another 13 cards and then place the last 13 cards face-down in a pile on the table **without dealing them out**. (*NOTE: The Aces are now at the bottom of the first pile dealt out in the order from the top of AC – AH – AS – AD and the bridged card is at the bottom of the last 13 card packet placed on the table.*)

8. You now need to organise the pack to allow for the spelling out of the spectator's thought-of Ace. Your aim is to get the pile with the bridged card at the bottom (the last pile placed on the table and which is Pile 4) on top of the first pile dealt (which has the Aces at the bottom and which is Pile 1) or, alternatively, to get Pile 4 to the bottom of the re-constituted pack with Pile 1 at the top of the pack with the other two piles (Pile 2 and Pile 3) in any order between them. This can be achieved as follows:

a. Invite the spectator to choose any two piles:

-   If the spectator chooses Pile 1 and either Pile 2 or
    Pile 3 place Pile 1 on the other chosen pile and
    the other pile on Pile 4.

-   If the spectator chooses Pile 4 and Pile 1 place
    Pile 4 on Pile 1 and then place Pile 2 on Pile 3 or
    Pile 3 on Pile 2.

-   If the spectator chooses Pile 2 and Pile 3 place
    either one on the other and then Pile 4 on Pile
    1.

b. Allow the spectator now to choose any of the
    combined piles:

-   If the spectator chooses the pile that does **not**
    contain the bridged card place the pile the
    spectator has chosen on the top or the bottom of
    the other pile as directed by the spectator.

-   If the spectator chooses the pile **with the bridged
    card at the bottom** – the other pile is placed on
    the top or bottom of the pile with the bridged
    card at the bottom.

-   If the spectator chooses the pile **containing the
    bridged card and the Aces** that pile is placed on
    the top, or the bottom, of the other pile.

c. Cutting the bridged card to the bottom of the
    reconstituted pack sets the pack with Pile 1 (with the
    Aces) at the top of the pack.

9. It is now possible for the spectator to spell out his or her thought-of Ace from the face-down pack using the following spelling-out procedure taking a card off the top of the pack for each letter.

    a. "A – C – E – O – F – C – L – U – B – S"
        The AC is at the "S" of the spelling

    b. "A – C – E – O – F – H – E – A – R – T – S"
        The AH is at the "S" of the spelling

    c. "A – C – E – O – F – S – P – A – D – E – S"
        The AS is the next card in the pack, ie. the top card of the remainder of the pack.

    d. "A – C – E – O – F – D – I – A – M – O – N – D – S"
        The AD is at the "S" of the spelling.

10. If you have chosen to perform the trick without the use of a bridged card proceed as follows:

    a. Extract the four Aces from the pack and place them face-up on the table as described at paragraph 1 above.

    b. Shuffle the rest of the pack and allow the spectator to shuffle the pack. As you take the pack back from the spectator glimpse and note the identity of the bottom card of the pack.

    c. Instruct the spectator to look at the Aces and to think of and remember any one of them.

d. Collect the Aces together and turn them face down (*NOTE: They should now be from the top AC – AH – AS – AD.*)

e. Deal off from the top of the rest of the face-down pack two hands each of 12-cards. Place the remainder of the pack to one side (*NOTE: Your noted card is the bottom card of this packet.*)

f. Invite the spectator to choose any one of the two face-down hands you have just dealt. Take the hand that has **not** been chosen and place it face-down on top of the cards you put aside at paragraph 10e above and take the hand that has been chosen and deal from it four 3-card packets: A – B – C – D from left to right.

g. Pick up the face-down Aces and place an Ace in turn from the top of the Ace packet on top of the packets A – B – C – D in that order. Then pick up the packets placing D on C, then DC on B, then DCB on A.

h. Hand the combined packet to the spectator and invite him or her to place it either on top or below the cards placed aside. He or she may then cut and complete the pack as many times as he or she wishes (*for an explanation of the term "cut and complete" see the "Introduction".*)

i. You then perform a Charlier Shuffle or mix, allowing the spectator to determine how many cards you take at each stage (*for details of how to perform this shuffle see the chapter on "Handling and Sleights-of-Hand".*)

At the conclusion of the shuffle the spectator may cut and complete the pack.

j. You now take the pack, turn it face-up and spread it to show the mix of the cards. In doing so you locate the card you noted at paragraph 10b above and split the pack at this point to make this card the bottom card of the pack when the pack is turned face-down.

k. Deal out the pack into four 13-card hands, dealing to each hand **consecutively** from the top of the face-down pack (*for an explanation of the term "dealing consecutively" see the "Introduction".*) You should note that the first hand you deal to will contain the Aces at the position to conclude the trick, ie. they are the bottom cards of the face-down hand in the order AC – AH – AS – AD. You now force the spectator to choose this hand using Magician's Choice (*for an explanation of the term "Magician's Choice" see the relevant section in the chapter "Handling and Sleights-of-Hand".*)

l. To do this proceed as follows:

- First place the face-down hands in a row A – B – C – D, where A is the first hand dealt.

- Invite the spectator to "Pick out two piles – touch the piles you want to pick out."

- If the spectator chooses any two of B, C, or D take the two chosen hands and place them aside. If the spectator chooses A and any one of B, C, or D take the hands **not** chosen from

B, C, and D and place them aside. In any case A and one other hand remain.

- Invite the spectator to "*Now* pick one of **those** piles."

- If the spectator chooses the pile other than A place that pile aside. If the spectator chooses Pile A place the other pile aside. In any case, pile A is left for the conclusion of the trick.

- Give the face-down hand to the spectator to spell out his or her thought-of Ace using the spelling-out procedure described at paragraph 9 above.

"A Magic Number"

Effect

A spectator has a free (secret) choice of a card from a hand of eight cards dealt to him or her from a shuffled pack. The spectator returns the cards, including the selected card, to the pack which is then shuffled. The performer then, using the pack, proceeds to arrive at a "magic number" which the spectator may, if he or she wishes, change by using the pack again. Once the spectator has arrived at a number he or she wishes to use the performer counts that many cards off the pack and arrives at the selected card.

Performance

1. Allow the spectator to shuffle and cut the pack as he or she wishes. Finally, you take the pack and cut it, taking the bridged card to the bottom of the pack. If you are not using a bridged card, when you take the pack from the spectator glimpse and take note of the bottom card of the pack.

2. Now deal off from the top of the face-down pack eight face-down cards and invite the spectator, if he or she wishes, to exchange any of the cards for others from the pack.

3. Instruct the spectator to shuffle or mix the cards and to make a secret note of the top card of the face-down packet.

4. As he or she does so give the rest of the pack an over-hand shuffle, bringing the bridged card from the bottom of the pack to the top of the pack (*for details on how to do this see the relevant section in the chapter "Handling and*

Sleights-of-Hand".) Alternatively, cut and complete the pack, open the pack at the bridged card and allow this card to drop onto the top of the bottom packet before taking that packet to the top of the pack (*for a definition of the term "cut and complete" see the "Introduction".*) If you are not using a bridge card, transfer the bottom card to the top of the pack using a controlled cut (*for details of how to perform this move see the relevant section in the chapter "Handling and Sleights-of-Hand".*) Alternatively, use a modified Charlier Cut or mix to transfer the card from the bottom to the top of the pack (*for details of how to do this see the relevant section in the chapter "Handling and Sleights of Hand".*)

5. The spectator now places his or her packet of cards face-down either on the top or bottom of the face-down pack and cuts and completes the pack, at will. You take the pack and mix the cards using a Charlier Shuffle. The spectator then cuts and completes the pack, at will. Finally, you cut the bridged card to the bottom of the pack. If you are not using a bridged card in the performance of the trick after the Charlier Shuffle and the spectator's cuts you turn the pack face-up and spread it to show the mix of the cards. Note the position of the card you identified at paragraph 1 above and cut the pack to place this card and the cards below it at the bottom of the face-down pack. (*For details of how to perform the Charlier Shuffle see the relevant section in the chapter "Handling and Sleights-of-Hand".*)

6. You now explain that you are going to arrive at "a magic number" by using cards from the pack. You explain that you will do this by dealing out face-up cards from the top of the pack in a line counting down from the top of the

line from 10 to 1, ie. "10", "9", "8", "7", etc. If there is a coincidence of the values of the card with the number you will stop the line at that card and start another line. If there is no coincidence of value and number you will close that line by taking the next card in the pack and placing it face-down on the line of face-up cards. You then begin another line. You will do this until you have counted out four lines. You will then add up the values of the cards at the end of the lines that have not been closed off. This is "the magic number".

7.   Demonstrate the procedure as you describe it, telling the spectator that the court cards (ie. Jacks, Queens, Kings) can be given any value – but that once this value is assigned to them then those cards retain that value throughout the dealing out.

8.   After the demonstration gather up the cards that have been dealt out and allow the spectator to shuffle them. Then place them face-down on top of the face-down pack.

9.   Now go through this process again, after inviting the spectator to fix the value to be used for the court cards.

10. When you have "the magic number" ask the spectator if he or she is happy with it or would he or she like to go through the procedure again to find another number. Do as the spectator wishes.

11. Once you have "the magic number" count off from the top of the face-down cards you have left in the pack to that number. The card at that number will be the card selected by the spectator.

"Real Magic"

EFFECT

From a shuffled and cut pack the spectator cuts off about half of the pack, shuffles it, and then counts the number of cards that have been cut off. The spectator now adds together the two digits of this number to arrive at a single digit number. The spectator then shuffles the cards he or she has cut off and then deals out cards from the packet equal to this number and secretly notes the card at that number. The spectator then shuffles the remaining cards in the packet, reconstitutes the packet and adds it to the shuffled remainder of the pack. The performer then proceeds to spell out a magic phrase, revealing the spectator's selected card on completion of the spelling-out.

PERFORMANCE

1. Allow the spectator to shuffle the pack and to cut and complete it, at will. (*For an explanation of the term "cut and complete" see the "Introduction".*)

2. When the spectator has completed his or her cutting, take the face-down pack and cut the bridged card to the bottom of the pack. If you are not using a bridge card proceed directly to paragraph 3 below.

3. Place the pack face-down on the table and invite the spectator to cut off about the top half of the pack, to shuffle the cards taken off, and then to count how many cards he or she has cut off by dealing them out in a pile face-down on the table. Encourage the spectator to take a reasonable number of cards but stress that he or she may

take less than half or more if he or she so wishes. (*NOTE:*
The trick will work for any number of cards from 10 to 49.)

4. You should note the number of cards counted out by the
    spectator.

5. You now instruct the spectator to add together the two
    digits of the number to arrive at an "arbitrary" number.
    You also announce that you now intend to produce some
    "real magic".

6. When the "arbitrary" number has been arrived at instruct
    the spectator to shuffle the cards he or she has just counted
    and then to deal off face-down in a pile on the table the
    number of cards corresponding to the "arbitrary" number.
    When the spectator has done so instruct him or her to
    (secretly) note the card at that number, to shuffle the rest
    of the cards, and to place them face-down on top of the
    cards on the table. (*NOTE: This places these cards on top of*
    the noted card.)

7. You now hand the spectator the rest of the pack and tell
    him or her to shuffle it.

8. You take these cards back and, if you are using a bridged
    card you cut that card to the bottom after shuffling the
    cards yourself. If you are not using a bridged card, you
    shuffle the cards yourself and note the card at the bottom
    of the pack after the shuffle. The spectator now places the
    cards on the table face-down either on top or below the
    rest of the pack and cuts and completes, at will. Finally,
    you cut the bridged card to the bottom of the pack or, if
    you are not using a bridged card, spread the pack face-up

to show the mix, and cut your noted card to place it at the bottom of the pack.

9. You can now spell out, as appropriate, from the top of the face-down pack the phrase to reveal the spectator's noted card. The spelling system is as follows:

a. **10–19 cards taken:** Spell out, taking a card for each letter, "M – A – G – I – C   C – A – R – D – S", *and take the card at the last letter of the spelling.*

b. **20 – 29 cards taken:** Spell out, taking a card for each letter, "N – O – W   F – O – R   S – O – M – E   R – E – A – L   M – A – G – I – C", *and take the card at the last letter of the spelling.*

c. **30 – 39 cards taken:** Spell out, taking a card for each letter, "N – O – W   F – O – R   S – O – M – E   R – E – A – L   M – A – G – I – C   H – E – Y   P – R – E – S – T – O", *and take the card at the last letter of the spelling.*

d. **40 – 49 cards taken:** Spell out, taking a card for each letter, "N – O – W   F – O – R   S – O – M – E   R – E – A – L   M – A – G – I – C   H – E – Y   P – R – E – S – T – O   A – N – D   S – H – A – Z – A – M", *and take the card at the last letter of the spelling.*

THE TWO-PACK TRICK

"Nobody Knows Anything"

EFFECT

Both packs are thoroughly shuffled and cut. The spectator then places a selected card between blocks of cards cut off from both packs. The spectator cuts this combined packet as many times as he or she wishes. The performer takes the packet and divides it into two parts, which are shuffled by the spectator and by the performer. There then follows a series of cuts and shuffles and mixing of the cards to produce a packet of indiscriminately mixed face-up and face-down cards. When the packet is given a final shuffle all the face-down cards are seen to be a mix of the two back colours. When the face-up cards are turned over all the backs are of one back colour except for one which is of the opposite colour and which, when it is turned face-up, is revealed as the spectator's selected card.

PERFORMANCE

1. Hand the Blue pack to the spectator and allow him or her to shuffle and cut it, at will.

2. When the spectator has finished take the Blue pack, shuffle it and cut and complete. Then turn the pack face-up and

spread it to show the mix of the cards. Finally, cut the face-up pack and note the identity of the card that, when you turn the pack face-down, will be the bottom card of the face-down pack. Turn the pack face-down and place it on the table. (*For an explanation of the term "cut and complete" see the "Introduction".*)

3. Now hand the Red pack to the spectator and instruct him or her to shuffle and cut it, at will.

4. When the spectator has finished take the Red pack, shuffle it and cut and complete. Then turn the pack face-up and spread it to show the mix of the cards. In doing so, locate the position of the card you identified at paragraph 2 (ie. the card that is the bottom card of the Blue pack) and split the pack at this point in such a way that that card will be the top card of the Red pack when that pack is turned face-down. Turn the pack face-down and place it on the table.

5. Invite the spectator to take whichever pack he or she wishes and to place it face-down in front of himself or herself.

6. If the spectator has taken the Blue pack (the pack with your noted card as its bottom card) instruct him or her to cut off about $^1/_3$ of the cards from the top of the pack and to place them face-down on the table. You then invite the spectator to take any card he or she wishes from **within** the Red pack, to note it secretly, and to place it face down on top of the cards he or she has just cut off the other pack. Having done this, the spectator cuts off about $^1/_3$ of the cards from what is left of the other pack (the Blue

pack) and places these cards on top of the selected card. He or she then cuts off about $^1/_3$ of the cards from the top of the Red pack and places these cards on top of the packet containing the selected card. He or she may now cut and complete the cards, at will.

7. If the spectator takes the Red pack (the pack with your noted card as the top card) instruct him or her to take out any card from **within** that pack, note it secretly, and to place it face-down on the table. The spectator then cuts off about 1/3 of the cards from the other pack (the Blue pack), places them face-down on the table, and places the selected card face-down on top of them. The spectator now cuts off about $^1/_3$ of what is left of the Blue pack and places these cards on top of the selected card. He or she then cuts off about $^1/_3$ of the Red pack and places these cards on top of the packet containing the selected card. The spectator may now cut and complete the cards, at will.

8. Having put aside the cards from both packs not used in either paragraph 6 or paragraph 7 above, you take the mixed card packet and cut it a few more times.

9. You then turn the packet face-up and spread it to show the mix of the cards. In doing so you note the location of the card you identified at paragraphs 2 and 4 above and cut the packet so that when the packet is face-down this card will be the top card of the packet. Having done this you place the packet face-down on the table.

10. You now cut the packet at about half-way down. Turn the cards that you have cut off face-up and hand them to the spectator. Instruct the spectator to shuffle the cards.

11. Turn the cards left on the table face-up and shuffle them yourself.

12. Now cut-off about half of the cards you have, turn them over, and hand them to the spectator. Instruct the spectator to cut off about half of the cards he or she has, to turn them over, and hand them to you. You both then shuffle the cards you have been given into the cards you have left. Repeat this procedure TWO more times.

13. When this has been done instruct the spectator to place his or her cards on the table. **Turn over the cards you have** and place them on top of the spectator's cards. The spectator may then cut and complete at will.

14. Take the packet from the table, **turn it over**, cut it into roughly equal parts and then shuffle the two parts together. Now spread out the cards to show the mix of face-up cards and Blue and Red face-down cards in the packet. Point out that nobody could now know which cards are face-up and which cards are face-down.

15. Then deal out the pack, dealing the face-up cards into one pile and the face-down cards into a second pile. The face-down pack should contain face-down cards of both back colours. Point this out and then turn over the face-up pile and spread it out. All the face-down cards will be of one colour – except for one card which will be of the other colour. Turn this card over to reveal the card selected by the spectator at paragraph 6–7 above.

(*NOTE: You should ensure at paragraph 12 that the spectator* ***does not turn over*** *the cards into which he or she is shuffling the cards you have passed to him or her.*)

THE FINAL TRICKS

"Same Number – Same Card"
(for one spectator)

EFFECT

The picture or court cards are taken out of the pack. A spectator is asked to choose any one of them. It is placed face-up on the table and the spectator assigns to it any value from 1–10. The pack is then cut by the spectator and from the pack is then extracted a sequence of cards using the value given by the spectator to the court card as the start of the sequence. The total value of the extracted cards and the value given to the court card is determined and a note is taken of this total and of the identity of the final card arrived at. The process is then repeated two more times. In every case the spectator allocates a different value to the court card. However, in every case the total arrived at and the final card of the sequence will be the same.

PERFORMANCE

1. In the routine this trick will normally follow the trick *"Nobody Knows Anything"*. However, if you have chosen not to perform this trick it will follow either *"Divination"* or *"Real Magic"*. Depending upon which trick it follows proceed as described below:

a. If the trick follows *"Nobody Knows Anything"* you will have on the table a mixture of two packs, some cards face-up and some cards face-down. Instruct the spectator to collect one of the packs, to order it face-down, and to replace it in its carton. You collect the other pack. As you do so ensure that you have from 10 to Ace in the bottom half of the pack. When the spectator has finished with the other pack, hand the top half of your pack to him or her to extract the court cards from it. You do likewise with your half. As you do so, order the bottom cards of your face-down half from 10 to Ace in that order. Then take the **non-court cards** from the spectator and place them face-down on top of your face-down packet.

b. If the trick follows on from *"Divination"* you already have the basis of the order of cards you require at the bottom of the face-down pack in the cards you are holding. In fact, you will have two sequences of cards that could be used as the basis. If the sequences have one or more court cards in them extract these cards and place them aside. As you do so, order one of the sequences from 10 to Ace and randomly disturb the order of the other sequence. With the packet face-down place the 10 to Ace sequence at the bottom of the packet (the suits are immaterial). You may, of course, have two sequences of 10 to Ace in your hand. In which case you merely order one of them appropriately and randomly disturb the order of the other sequence. Finally, if you find that you require cards to complete a sequence of 10 to Ace then the necessary cards are in the discard pile from the trick *"Divination"*. In this case, instruct the spectator to gather up the discard pile, to extract the court cards from it and place them aside, and to hand you the other cards, which you can then use to complete your sequence. In all cases, you instruct the spectator to shuffle the cards he or she has and to hand them to you. Again, in all cases, you will finish with a face-down pack with the bottom ten cards in the sequence 10 to Ace in that order.

c. If the trick follows *"Real Magic"* hand about half of the cards to the spectator, who should extract the court cards, place them aside, and shuffle the remaining cards. Meanwhile, you extract the court cards from your half of the pack, place them aside, and, in doing so, as far as you are able, create a 10 to Ace sequence in the other cards. In discarding the court cards place them in a random face-up / face-down order. Take the shuffled cards from the spectator and hand him or her the face-up / face-down cards. Instruct the spectator to go through them to ensure that there are no non-court cards among them. This should provide sufficient distraction to allow you to complete your 10 to Ace sequence and place it at the bottom of the face-down pack.

2. By whatever means you have achieved it, you now have a face-down pack (less the court cards) with the bottom ten cards ordered from 10 to Ace. Instruct the spectator to choose any one of the court cards, to place the chosen card face-up on the table, and to assign to it any value from 1 to 10. He or she should make a note of or remember this number.

3. You now invite the spectator to cut and complete the face-down pack. (*For an explanation of the term "cut and complete" see the "Introduction".*)

4. You then take the pack and count off from the top of it a number of cards equal to the value the spectator has assigned to the court card. As the cards are counted their order is not reversed, ie. each card is counted off beneath the preceding card. The packet that is counted off is turned face-up to reveal the face card of the packet and the packet is then placed face-up on the court card so that only the left hand index of the court card can be seen. You then use the value of the face card of the packet as the number of cards you next count off the top of the pack. This packet is placed on the preceding packet as described above and the process is continued through the pack, until you reach the final card of the pack or until there are insufficient cards left in the pack to match the value of the face-card of the packet.

5. The values of all the revealed cards and the value assigned to the initial face-up card are now added together.

6. The spectator is instructed to note and remember this number and to note and remember the identity of the revealed card.

7. Having arrived at the total, you collect up all the cards from left to right, sliding each card or packet beneath the subsequent card or packet, and then place the pack face-down on the table, or the cards you have collected up face-down on the face-down cards you have left over from the counting-out.

8. Now repeat the process described in paragraphs 4–6 above, having forecast that you will arrive at the same total and the same final card, and having allowed the spectator to assign a different number from 1 to 10 to the court card, which you take from the top of the pack and place face-up on the table. You will arrive at the same total and at the same final card.

9. Collect up the cards as before, place the court card face-up on the table, and instruct the spectator to assign yet another value from 1 to 10 to it. Then go through the counting-out procedure again and once again arrive at the same total and the same final card.

"Everybody Shouts"
(for two or more spectators)

Effect
(Using a bridged card)

A number of spectators in turn are handed the pack and told to shuffle it. The performer then takes the pack and asks the first spectator to take the top card of the pack, secretly note it, and then shuffle it back into the pack. This procedure is repeated for any number of spectators. When all the spectators have taken and noted a card the performer deals out the same number of cards as there are spectators who have taken a card. The spectators look at these cards and confirm that their cards are there. The performer takes the cards and places them face-up on the table in a row. The performer then asks the spectators at a given signal to shout out the name of their card and to pick the card up from the table. They all shout out and attempt to pick up the same card at the given signal.

Effect
(Not using a bridged card)

The trick begins and ends as described above for the bridged card, the difference being the series of cuts and deals leading to the selection of the spectators' cards.

Performance
(Using a bridged card)

1. Each spectator involved is handed the pack in turn and instructed to shuffle it.

2. You take the pack back, shuffle it, and cut at the bridged card, allowing the bridged card to fall on top of the packet that will be the top of the whole pack when you complete the cut and the cards are turned face-down.

3. You invite one of the spectators to take the top card of the face-down pack, note it secretly without revealing it either to you or to any other spectator, and then to shuffle it back into the pack.

4. You take the pack back, shuffle it, and then cut the bridged card to the bottom of the pack. The next spectator is then invited to take the bottom card, note it secretly without revealing it either to you or any other spectator, and then to shuffle it back into the pack.

5. You repeat paragraphs 2 and 3 and paragraphs 2 and 4 alternately until all the spectators involved have taken and selected a card.

6. Once the final spectator has noted a card and shuffled it back into the pack, you take the pack back, shuffle it and cut at the bridged card, allowing the bridged card to fall on top of the packet that will be the top of the whole pack when you complete the cut and the pack is face-down.

7. Now deal out, face-down onto the table as many cards as there are spectators who have taken and noted a card. Having done so, pick up the cards and mix them. With the cards still face-down hand the packet to each spectator in turn and ask them to confirm that their card is in the packet.

8. You now take the packet and spread it out face-up on the table. You instruct the spectators on your count of "1–2–3" to shout out the name of their card and pick it up. They will all shout out and attempt to pick up the same card (the bridged card).

Performance
(Not using a bridged card)

1. Each spectator involved is handed the pack and instructed to shuffle it.

2. You take the pack back, shuffle it, place it face-down on the table and instruct the first spectator to take the top card. Instruct him or her to note it secretly without revealing it either to you or to any of the other spectators. When he or she has done so ask him or her to place the card face-down on top of the face-down pack.

3. A second spectator is instructed to cut off about half of the pack, which he or she should place face-down on the table. Now instruct the spectator to take the bottom part of the pack, turn it face-up, and place it on top of the packet he or she has just cut off. Finally, you instruct him or her to turn over the whole pack.

4. You now take the pack, without turning it over or disturbing it in any way, and cut it in exactly the same way as the spectator, including the final turning over of the pack. When you make your initial cut off the top of the pack you should ensure that you are cutting **below** the level at which the spectator cut. (*For a full description and explanation of this handling see the relevant section in the chapter "Handling and Sleights-of-Hand".*)

5. When you have completed the whole procedure you place the pack in front of the second spectator and instruct him or her to take the first face-down card in the pack. He or she should note the card secretly without revealing it to either you or another spectator.

6. When the spectator has done this instruct him or her to place the card face-down on the table, to turn any face-up cards in the pack face-down, and to place the face-down pack on top of it.

7. You take the face-down pack, cut off about the top ¾ of the cards, turn these cards over and place them at the bottom of the pack. You then turn the pack over, cut off about the top ½ of the cards, turn these cards over and place them at the bottom of the pack. You turn the pack over and spread it until you sight the first face-up card. You cut the pack at this point leaving the face-down card above the face-up card in place. The other face-down cards above that card you turn and place at the bottom of the pack. You now place the pack on the table and instruct the third spectator to take the top card of the pack and to note it secretly without revealing it to either you or another spectator.

8. When the spectator has done this instruct him or her to place the card on top of the face-down pack. Immediately, turn to the fourth spectator and ask him or her how many cards between 10 and 20 he or she wants you to deal off the pack. Deal off face-down onto the table the required number of cards into a pile, and instruct the spectator to cut off from the top of this pile as many cards as he or she wishes, and immediately either put them in a pocket or hide them. Point out that this is because you do not want to know how many cards have been cut and you do not want the spectator to know now many cards he or she has cut off. When the spectator has made the cut and hidden the cards ask how many cards he or she would now like you to deal off the pack. Deal off face-down onto the face-down cards left on the table the required number of cards and instruct the spectator to repeat the procedure of cutting off a number of cards from the pile and hiding them with the cards already cut off. You now pick up the cards left in the pile on the table and, without disturbing their order, place them on top of the pack. You then immediately deal out into a face-down pile on the table a number of cards that is the total of the cards dealt in the two previous deals. You do this without counting them out aloud or stating the number.

9. You now instruct the spectator to take all the cards he or she has cut off and to count them. You tell him or her that you will use this number to determine how many cards are cut off the packet you have just dealt out. While the spectator is counting the cut-off cards pick up the pile you have dealt onto the table and place it on the top of the pack. When the spectator has completed the count take his or her cards and place them at the bottom of the pack.

You then count off a number of cards from the top of the pack corresponding to the number he or she counted. These cards are transferred to the bottom of the pack. The spectator is instructed to take the top card of the pack. He or she should note it secretly without revealing it to either you or any other spectator.

10. When the spectator has done this instruct him or her to place the card face-down on top of the face-down pack. If more spectators are to be involved in the trick you should go through the sequence of procedures described in paragraphs 3-9 above again to the point at which all the spectators have taken out and noted a card. *The final spectator to take a card should replace it on **the top** of the face-down pack.*

11. In taking the pack back note the identity of the bottom card of the pack. Having done so, allow each of the spectators who are taking part in the trick to cut and complete (*for an explanation of the term "cut and complete" see the "Introduction".*) You then take the pack, turn it face-up and spread the cards to show the mix of the cards. Note the location of your noted card and cut the pack to place this card at the bottom of the face-down pack.

12. Once this has been done you should proceed as described at paragraphs 7 and 8 above for the performance using a bridged card.

HANDLING AND
SLEIGHTS-OF-HAND

This chapter deals with the techniques that can be used to manipulate and control the cards. It is not intended that the newcomer to card magic should work methodically through the material studying and practising each technique. Such a procedure would not only be counter-productive but also boring in the extreme. Rather what is intended is that the reader should use the chapter as a reference source on the various techniques, turning to it as required during the study of the various tricks and for this reason extensive references are made to this chapter in the descriptions of the performance of the tricks. However, the beginner is strongly advised to master at the very outcome a number of essential skills. These are:

The Overhand Shuffle and Controls
The Riffle Shuffle and Controls
A False Shuffle
A False Cut

With regard to the use of the techniques a word of warning is appropriate: **do not over-use them**. They do allow you to create the illusion of the cards being indiscriminately mixed. They do allow you to place cards in positions in a pack or packet that facilitate an effect. However, if they are used when they are not essential (either as a habit or to give you a degree of personal satisfaction in deluding the audience) their very use will give rise to suspicion and the spectators, seeing the moves used so often, will begin to look carefully at them and thus might detect the subterfuge involved.

In the descriptions of the pre-arranged pack tricks in the relevant chapter points at which false shuffles and false mixes might be used are given. In the description of the tricks in the other chapters it has been left to the discretion of the performer as to when it is appropriate to use them.

Finally, you should note that the use of certain techniques would allow for the performance of a trick to be adapted or simplified. For example, in the final trick *"Everybody Shouts"* the bridged card is used to great effect. However, it might be considered that it is used too frequently. The presentation could be improved by alternating the use of the bridged card with controlled shuffles and false mixes to present the cards to be selected. Similarly, in the performance of the trick without the use of a bridged card, these techniques could be used to replace, enhance, or simplify the series of forces used to present the card to be selected.

Practise the techniques to the point at which they are almost automatic in performance and do not look at your hands when performing then. If you look at your hands the chances are that the spectators will too and what would go unobserved will be closely examined.

The Overhand Shuffle

Hold the pack, face-down, with the outer end towards the spectators. The cards' outer sides should rest on the part of the palm at the junction between the palm and the fingers at an angle of about 45°, the inner side upward. The thumb rests across the top card of the pack, and the first finger is against the outer corner. The other fingers rest on the face of the bottom card.

Using the hand not holding the pack lift up the bottom half or so of the pack with the thumb holding the inner end of the packet and the first three fingers at the outer end.

Move the packet over the top of the other packet and pull off from the top of it single cards or clumps of cards with the thumb of the hand holding what was the top part of the pack, allowing the cards or single card to fall onto that packet as the packet in the other hand is moved backwards and forwards.

Carry on with this procedure until all the cards have been pulled off what was the bottom of the pack onto what was the top of the pack.

To continue the shuffle, again cut away the bottom half or so of the pack and go through the procedure gain.

CONTROLLING THE CARDS

The top card can be taken to the bottom of the pack by slipping the card off the top of the pack as the shuffle begins and immediately shuffling off the rest of the pack onto it, ie. the whole pack other than the top card is lifted to begin the shuffle.

The bottom card of the pack can be moved to the top of the pack by beginning the shuffle by lifting about the bottom $^2/_3$ of the pack. This packet is held between the thumb at the inner end and the second and third fingers at the outer end. As the shuffle progresses pressure is exerted on the final card in the packet to ensure that it is the final card shuffled off.

To hold the bottom card at the bottom of the pack the shuffle begins by lifting the packet which will be shuffled off from the middle of the pack and allowing the top and bottom remaining packets to fall together.

To transpose the top and bottom cards of the pack begin by slipping the top card as described above for taking the top card to the bottom. Then shuffle off all the other cards onto it exerting pressure on the final card (what was the bottom card of the pack) to ensure that this card is the final card shuffled off.

The Riffle Shuffle and Controls

Hold the pack face-down with the outer side of the pack towards the spectators. The pack is held with both hands, the thumbs at the inner side and the fingers at the outer side.

Split the pack into two halves, moving the top half to the left and the bottom half to the right, and place the two halves face-down on the table end to end, the outer sides of the packets still towards the spectators.

Move the two packets against each other until the two inner corners are touching and form the point a V with the open end of the V facing the spectators.

Change the position of the hands holding the packets so that the thumbs are immediately behind the corners forming the point of the V, the little fingers at the corners of the outside ends, the first fingers pressing down on the packets at the open part of the V. The little fingers are pushing at the end outside corners. The other fingers are at the outer sides of the packets.

Push down with all the fingers and at the same time lift the inner sides off the table with the thumbs, keeping the two corners forming the sharp end of the V in close contact.

Allow the cards to fall away in a cascade from the bottom of each packet interleaving with each other as they fall.

Close the V by pushing the inner ends of the two packets together thus completely inter-weaving them.

Push the two packets into each other and square up the pack.

CONTROLLING THE CARDS

To retain the top card or a top block of cards at the top of the shuffled pack control the release of the left hand packet (ie. what was the top half of the pack) so that the desired card or cards drop last.

To retain the bottom card or a bottom block of cards at the bottom of the shuffled pack allow the bottom card or the bottom cards of the right hand packet (ie. what was the bottom half of the pack) to fall first.

The Charlier Shuffle and Controls

With the outer ends of the cards facing the spectators, the pack is placed face-down diagonally across the up-turned palm immediately adjoining the base of the fingers. The thumb is at the outer side of the pack towards the outer corner and the tips of the fingers curl around the inner side.

The basic shuffle (or, rather, mix) begins by the other hand (palm down) moving over the pack. The thumb of this hand is at the inner end of the pack with the tip of the third finger curling over the outer end towards the inner corner. The pack is then tilted, the outer side of the pack pivoting on the upturned palm of the up-turned hand.

The upper hand now slides out a small packet of cards from the **bottom** of the pack, leaving the remainder of the pack resting on the fingers of the lower hand, the thumb of which moves onto the top of the pack.

This thumb now pushes off a small packet of cards from the **top** of what was the pack and these cards are slid **beneath** the cards held in the other hand.

The fingers of the other hand now push off a small packet of cards from the **bottom** of what was the pack and these cards are placed on the **top** of the cards already taken off the pack.

This alternating top and bottom extraction of cards is continued until all the cards that constituted the original pack have been transferred and the shuffle (or mix) is complete. The rule to be remembered is that cards taken from the bottom go on top, and cards taken from the top go to the bottom.

CONTROLLING THE CARDS

Although the cards appear to have been thoroughly mixed the outcome of the shuffle is the same as would have resulted if the pack had been cut and completed. So, if at the end of the shuffle you cut the original bottom card of the pack back to the bottom of the pack then the pack will be back in its original order. Alternatively, if you had started with a bridged card at the bottom of the pack and if you cut it back to the bottom of the pack after the shuffle you would restore the pack to its original order.

Another method of controlling the mix when using a small packet of cards is to note the number of cards being transferred during the mix and then to perform a second mix transferring the same sequence of cards but this time starting the mix from the top of the pack. For example, if on the first mix of a 12-card packet you take four cards off the bottom, three off the top, two off the bottom, leaving three cards to be placed at the bottom and you then on the second mix take four cards off the top, three off the bottom, two off the top, leaving three cards to be placed on the top, the pack will be back in its original order. It might be thought that such handling would be immediately noted by the spectators but if it is done boldly and quickly it will be accepted as a fair mix of the packet.

Creating and Handling a Bridged Card

There are a number of ways in which the bottom card of the pack may be handled to produce a convex bridge.

For the first, hold the pack face down with the outer end towards the spectators. The thumb is positioned on the outer side and the fingers wrap around the inner side. Move the other hand over the pack, the thumb at the inner end of the pack and the fingers at the outer end, and lift the pack very slightly, allowing the bottom card to fall onto and rest on the palm of the hand originally holding the pack, the separation of the card being facilitated by a slight upward pressure by the thumb of the upper hand on the rest of the pack, and the procedure being concealed by tilting the pack, ie. raising the inner end. Squeeze the card at its sides using the fingers of the lower hand to press the card against the fleshy part of the palm at the base of the thumb of the same hand. Only very slight pressure to produce a very slight bridge is required. Then allow the pack to drop back onto the card. The bottom card is bridged along its length with a convex bridge.

For the second, again hold the pack face-down with the outer end towards the spectators. The pack rests on the palm of the hand with the thumb at the outer side and the fingers wrapped around the inner side. The other hand moves over the pack and lifts it leaving the bottom card in the palm of the hand originally holding the pack. The pack is then turned so that the inner side points downwards towards the single card. The cards are then allowed to fall in a cascade onto the single card which is held between the fingers and thumbs of the lower hand. This will produce a "round of applause" (ie. the sound of cards falling onto the single card). More significantly, it produces a convex bridge of the card along its length.

A third method, which again allows you to bridge the card quite openly without raising any suspicion in the spectators, is to play with the pack in a very casual way while you are chatting with them. In doing so order the cards so that the card you wish to bridge is either the top card or bottom card of the face-down pack. When this has been achieved suddenly cut the pack into two roughly equal packets and hand the packet not containing the card you wish to bridge to a spectator, instructing him or her to shuffle it. While he or she is doing so you shuffle the packet you have retained to either take the top card to the bottom or the bottom card to the top and then back to the bottom, depending upon the initial position of the card you wish to bridge. At this point the spectator is likely to have completed his or her shuffle. Ask him or her to either give the packet another good shuffle or, if there is more than one spectator, to pass it to another spectator for them to shuffle. As this is being done turn your packet face-up and, while playing with the cards as you watch and chat with the spectator/s, take the top face-up card and, under cover of the hand not holding the packet, give that card a convex bridge along its length. Once you have done this cut the packet to place the bridged card roughly in the middle of the packet and turn the packet face-down. Now exchange packets with the spectator/s, instructing them to shuffle the second packet while you shuffle the other packet. The two packets are then placed together to reconstitute the pack (with somewhere within it your bridged card).

For some occasions (eg. the two pre-prepared (or "stacked") tricks of the routine) you are able to produce the bridged card prior to the performance in which you are going to use it. In which case, if the pre-prepared trick you are going to use it for allows it, once you have created the bridged card cut it into the middle of the pack before placing the pack in its carton.

You should note that only a very slight bridge is required to produce the desired outcome and that during performance (particularly after riffle shuffles) it may be necessary to "refresh" the bridge.

HANDLING A BRIDGED CARD

To cut the bridged card from within the pack hold the pack loosely, the outer end towards the spectators, with the face of the cards facing outwards and the backs inwards. The thumb is very loosely on the top side of the pack and the fingers are gently supporting the bottom side from beneath. The other hand (again very gently) rests on the pack, the thumb at the inside end and the fingers at the outer end. The pressure of the thumb on the top side of the pack is relaxed, and the pack is allowed to open at the natural break. The bottom section of the pack will fall into the palm of the hand. You lift away this bottom packet of the pack and place it face-down on top of the pack. This should put the bridged card to the bottom of the re-constituted pack. It is prudent, however, to check that this has been achieved and this can be done by glimpsing the card at the bottom of the pack. To do this, after you have completed the cut, turn the face-down pack so that the backs of the cards are towards the spectators with the sides of the cards at top and bottom. Hold the pack with both hands, the back of the hands towards the spectators and with the thumbs on the face of the pack and the fingers on the back of the pack. Tap the bottom side of the pack on the table to square up the cards and, in doing so, glimpse the identity of the bottom card. Once you have done so turn the pack face-down and place it on the table. If you do not glimpse the required card have the pack cut again or cut the pack yourself and repeat the whole procedure.

To allow the pack to be cut and to then restore it to its original order begin with the bridged card at the bottom of the face-down pack and allow the pack to be cut and completed. Then cut the bridged card to the bottom of the pack as described in the previous paragraph. To control a selected card which has been returned to either the top or the bottom of the pack after the pack has been cut and completed begin with the bridged card either at the top or at the bottom of the pack and allow a spectator to replace his or her selected card on the top or at the bottom of the pack. Then allow the spectator to cut and complete the pack as many times as he or she wishes. If you then cut the bridged card to the bottom of the pack the selected card will be the top card of the pack.

To control a selected card returned to the "the middle of the pack" after the pack has been cut and completed begin with the bridged card at the bottom of the pack. Cut off the top half of the face-down pack and place it face-down on the table in front of the spectator. He or she places the selected card on top of this packet and you place what was the bottom half of the pack on top of the selected card. The spectator may now cut and complete, at will. Finally, you cut the bridged card to the bottom of the pack, which places the selected card at the top of the pack. Alternatively, with the pack in hand, cut off the top half of the pack with the other hand and hold this packet face-down towards the spectator for him or her to place the selected card on top of it. Then place what was the bottom of the pack face-down on top of the spectator's card. You then proceed as described above, allowing the spectator to cut and complete before you finally cut the bridged card to the bottom of the pack.

To disguise the use of a bridged card or to retain a card or block of cards at the top of the pack, having cut the bridged card to the bottom of the pack begin the procedure again. This time, in relaxing the pressure of the thumb on the top side of the pack, allow approximately the bottom $1/3$ of the pack to fall away into the palm. Now using the index finger of the other hand you open the top $^2/_3$ of the pack as if opening a book and insert what was the bottom $^1/_3$ of the pack into the gap thus formed and then close the pack. The bridged card is now approximately $^2/_3$ of the way down the pack. Repeat this procedure allowing the cards **below** the bridged card to fall into the palm of your hand. As you did before open up a gap in the other cards and place the cards from your palm in it. When the pack is closed the bridged card will be at the bottom of the pack.

False Cuts

If you are using a bridged card the illusion of a fair cut is easily achieved (beginning with the bridged card at the bottom of the pack) by casually cutting and completing the pack two or more times before cutting the bridged card to the bottom of the pack. If, however, you are not using a bridged card or if the bridged card is and must remain within the pack then the illusion must be achieved by other means. One straight-forward (but still deceptive) procedure is to begin with the pack face-down with the outer side towards the spectators. The pack is held with both hands, the thumbs at the inner side and the fingers at the outer side. Tilt the pack, raising the inner side with the thumbs, and then with the right hand pull the bottom $^1/_3$ of the pack to the right and place it face down on the top of the pack, out-jogged on the outer end of the pack by about half an inch. The consequent out-jog at the inner end of the pack is concealed by the back of the left hand. Repeat the movement for the next $^1/_3$ of the pack from the bottom of the pack – this time placing the cut-off packet directly on top of the out-jogged packet. Now push down with the left little finger on what is the concealed out-jogged bottom $^1/_3$ of the packet and pull that packet to the right under the pack with the right hand, placing it on the top of the pack. The pack is then in its original order. The procedure when performed quickly and slickly gives the illusion of a genuine cut.

A False Shuffle

The simplest false shuffle is what is normally described as the "optical shuffle". If it is performed confidently and smoothly, without looking at the hands or attracting the attention of the spectators to the hands, it is a very deceptive false shuffle. To perform it begin with the pack in position for an overhand shuffle as described earlier in this chapter. Cut away about the bottom $^2/_3$ of the pack and, as in the genuine overhand shuffle, move this packet over the top of the other packet. Do so until it completely covers the other packet without relaxing your grip of it. As the cut-away packet moves over the packet that was the top of the pack place the thumb of the hand holding this packet on top of the cut-off packet, then take the bottom $^2/_3$ you cut off upwards, as you do so allowing the thumb to slip along the top card of the upward moving packet **but do not release any cards from the packet**. Once the packet has cleared what was the bottom $^1/_3$ of the pack move it down behind that packet and allow a small block of cards to fall onto the bottom of that packet. Continue the procedure until all the cards from what was the bottom part of the pack have been placed behind what was the top $^1/_3$ of the pack. The illusion of a true shuffle can be heightened by, when the $^2/_3$ packet is moved behind the $^1/_3$ packet, the cards of the $^1/_3$ packet are allowed to tilt towards the thumb of the hand holding them.

Another straight-forward and effective false shuffle again begins with the cards in the position for an overhand shuffle. Take about the bottom ¾ of the pack and lift it above the other cards as if beginning a standard overhand shuffle. At the same time the thumb of the lower hand pulls the top ¼ of the pack down onto the fingers of that hand and moves this packet under what was the bottom ¾ of the pack. A break or gap is held between what was the upper ¼ of the pack and what was the bottom ¾ of the pack using the thumb and fingers of the hand holding the pack. Continue pulling off small blocks of cards from the top of what was the bottom ¾ of the pack, placing these blocks beneath what was the top ¼ of the pack, maintaining the gap or break. When all the cards have been transferred the pack will be back in its original order. The secret of success with this false shuffle (which is, in fact, a series of cuts off the top of the pack being transferred to the bottom of the pack in order) is to keep the gap or break as small as possible and to hide it with what was the bottom ¾ of the pack by tilting the pack towards the spectators. The illusion created is of the cards being shuffled into the bottom part of the pack.

A False Mix of the Pack

The impression can be given that a pack or block of cards is being thoroughly mixed when, in fact, no change is being made in its order. To do this begin with a bridged card at the bottom of the pack or packet and by then performing a Charlier Shuffle as described earlier in this chapter. You may, if you wish, during the shuffle allow a spectator to determine how many cards you take from the top and from the bottom of the pack or packet. Having completed the shuffle you place the pack face-down on the table, cut off the top ¾ of the pack, and place this packet by the side of what was the bottom of the pack (A). Now cut off the top ¾ of the packet you took off A and place these cards by the side of what was this packet (B). Now cut off the top half of the packet you have placed beside B and place it by the side of what was the bottom of this packet (C). The last packet is D. You now have on the table four packets D – C – B – A. Place A on D and B on AD and then BAD on C. Then perform a second Charlier Shuffle. Both you and the spectators may now cut and complete, at will. Finally, you cut the bridged card to the bottom of the pack and the pack is then back in its original order.

Transferring Bottom Card to Top by a Cut or a Mix

The most effective way to transfer the bottom card to the top of the pack is by an overhand shuffle (*see the relevant section earlier in this chapter*). However, it is possible to make the transfer by means of a cut. To do so begin with the face-down pack diagonally across the palm with the outer end towards the spectators. The pack should be tilted roughly at an angle of about 45° with the inner end raised. The thumb is at the outer side corner and the fingers wrap around the inner side from below, the little finger at the inner side corner. The other hand (palm down) is over the top of the pack with the fingers at the outer end and the thumbs at the inner end. The little finger of the lower hand pulls down on the inner corner of the bottom card of the pack to form a break (*for an explanation of this term see the "Introduction"*). As soon as the break is formed it is transferred immediately to the fleshy part of the top of the thumb of the upper hand as the bottom hand moves slightly outwards and away from the pack. This bottom hand now turns palm towards the outer side of the pack and using the middle finger at the outer end of the pack and the thumb at the inner end and extracts the middle third of the pack. As the packet is extracted it rests on the third and little finger and the index finger presses down on the packet. This grip allows the thumb to move onto the top of the packet to replace the index finger which moves to below the cards. The packet is now gripped by the thumb on top and all the fingers below. The fingers move under the packet to wrap around the inner side as the thumb slides to the outside corner – the packet now lies diagonally across the palm of the hand. The other (upper) hand now places its packet face-down on top of the packet. As it does so the thumb of the upper hand allows the card below the break to drop onto the lower packet, the card being guided onto the packet by the thumb and fleshy part of the palm below the thumb of the lower hand. Simultaneously, the thumb of the upper hand forms and holds a break at the inner end of the pack between the packet it holds and the bottom packet. The lower hand now moves away from the pack and then, turning palm towards the outer side of the pack, removes a block of cards from the middle of the pack above the break held by the thumb. This block of cards is placed on top of the pack. The cards that were below the break are then transferred to the top of the pack, which is then placed face-down on the table.

An alternative and much easier way to accomplish the same outcome is to use a Charlier-style mix. If it is used it should be done boldly and quickly, if possible while providing some distraction of the attention of the spectators. The handling required begins with the pack in position as for a "genuine" Charlier Shuffle or mix (*see the relevant section earlier in this chapter*). The cards are pushed off by the thumb from the top of the pack. They are pushed off individually until a small block is formed. This packet is then take by the other hand. This procedure continues through the pack, **the cards all being taken from the top of the pack**, alternating the placing of the packets above and below the cards already taken off. At the end of the procedure a small packet (of, say, 5 or 6 cards) is left of the original pack. All but the last of these cards are transferred below the cards already taken off and the last card is placed on top of the pack. The pack is then placed on the table.

Transferring Top Card to Bottom by a Cut or a Mix

Again the most effective way to transfer the card is by an overhand shuffle (*see the relevant section earlier in this chapter*), but also again it can be accomplished by a cut or a mix.

To perform the cut begin with the pack held as for the cutting procedure described in the previous section except that for this procedure the outer end of the pack should be slightly raised, and the break should be formed and held below the top card of the pack. Cut off the bottom ¼ of the pack and place these cards on top of the pack. Still holding the break cut off what is now the bottom ¼ of the pack and place these on top. Then take all the cards below the break and place these on top. End the cut by taking out about $1/3$ of the pack from the middle and placing these cards on top.

To accomplish the same outcome by means of a Charlier-style mix reverse the procedure described in the previous section, ie. the cards are taken from the bottom of the pack and the last card of the final packet is placed below the cards taken off.

The Cut Deeper Force

To force a card is, by concealed means, to ensure that a spectator receives or chooses a card or cards determined by the performer. A straight-forward, yet very effective, force for the top card of the pack, as developed by the card magician Ed Balucci, is the Cut Deeper Force. The force is accomplished by first cutting off about ¼ of the pack, turning this packet over, and placing it on top of the rest of the pack. The pack is then cut about ½ way down and this packet is turned over and placed on top of the other cards. The first face-down card in the pack is what was originally the top card of the pack. The deceptiveness of the procedure can be enhanced by allowing the spectator to make all the cuts.

The principle underlying the procedure can be adapted to meet any requirement. For example, if the top ¼ of the pack is cut off, turned over, and placed beneath the rest of the pack, and then the bottom ½ of the pack is cut-off, turned over, and placed on top of the pack, what was originally the bottom card of the pack will be the first face-up card in the pack. This procedure could be used at the conclusion of a trick to reveal a spectator's selected card that has been manipulated to the bottom of the pack.

Further variations of the principle are used in the trick *"Everybody Shouts"* when performed without the use of a bridged card (*see the previous chapter*). In the second variation the procedure is varied to force the bottom card of the pack **face-down**.

Magician's Choice

Magician's Choice (or, as it is sometimes referred to by the French word meaning ambiguous – "equivoque") is a means of producing the outcome in a spectator's choice of card or cards that is required by the performer. Its success depends upon the way in which the choice is presented to the spectator and the way in which the response is interpreted by the performer.

An example of a multiple choice illustrates the principle involved.

You begin by placing five cards or five packets of cards on the table – say A, B, C, D, and E, with A being the required card or packet. The spectator is asked to "pick out" any four cards or packets and to touch the cards or packets. If the spectator chooses B, C, D, and E you pick up those cards or packets and place them aside, leaving you with the required card or packet. If the spectator chooses A and three other cards or packets discard the card or packet he or she has not chosen and proceed to another choice. You now have on the table A and, say, B, C, and D, and you ask the spectator "now to choose any two of the four that are left". If the spectator chooses any two of B, C, or D discard those cards or packets, leaving A and one other card or packet. If the spectator chooses A and another card or packet, discard the other two cards or packets, again leaving A and one other card or packet. You now have A and one other card or packet on the table and you now ask the spectator "to pick out one of those cards / packets". If he or she chooses A then you discard the other card or packet. If he or she chooses the other card or packet you discard that. In any case, you finish with the required card on the table.

Sources and Background

A Basic Reference Library

I owe my own interest in card magic to the writers included in the short bibliography set out below, and, as will be obvious in the section that follows, the development of the tricks in this book would not have been possible without drawing heavily on their work. I take this opportunity to express my admiration of their contribution to the advancement of card magic and to express my gratitude to them for the pleasure and inspiration they have given to me over many years.

Jean Hugard and Frederick Braué
The Royal Road to Card Magic (Dover, New York, 1999)
Expert Card Technique (Dover, New York, 1974)

Jean Hugard and John J. Crimmins, Jnr
The Encyclopaedia of Card Tricks (Dover, New York, 1974)
(a revised edition with Index was published by Foulsham, Slough, 2003)

Karl Fulves
Self-Working Card Tricks (Dover, New York, 1976)
More Self-Working Card Tricks (Dover, New York, 1984)

Self-Working Close-up Card Magic (Dover, New York, 1995)

Self-Working Mental Magic (Dover, New York, 1979)

Martin Gardner

Mathematics, Magic, and Mystery (Dover, New York, 1956)

And for those who wish to develop further their repertoire and techniques the following books are recommended:

Arthur F. MacTier

Card Concepts (Davenport, London, 2000)

Simon Aronson

Bound To Please (Aronson, Chicago, 1994)

The Background to the Tricks

"THINK OF A CARD – SPELL ANOTHER"

The basis of this trick is *"Duo Spell"* in Karl Fulves's book *More Self-Working Card Tricks* (pages 126/7), which for its effect depends upon a procedure developed by Paul Swinford. The trick, as described by Fulves, begins with a pre-arranged (or "stacked") pack with two 8-card sequences on top of the pack: (QH, 6C, 2H, JS, 8S, KD, 3D, 4C and JD, 10C, AH, QC, 7S, 5D, 8D, 3S). These cards are delivered to two spectators by handing the first eight cards to the first spectator and the second eight cards to the second spectator. The cards are then displayed, without disturbing their order, and each spectator is invited to think of a card in the hand they have been shown other than the first and last card (ie. he or she can select from the middle six cards of the hand). The hands are then put together, placing the second hand on top of the first. The performer then carries out what Fulves calls "a reverse faro", that is the extraction from the combined packet of every alternate card. To do this the first card of the packet is out-jogged at the outer end about half the length of the card. This card, together with the second card underneath it is taken into the other hand. The procedure is repeated through the packet, taking each pair in turn under the previous pairs removed and placing them in alignment so that when you have gone through the packet cards 1, 3, 5, 7, 9, 11, 13, 15 are out-jogged outwards and cards 2, 4, 6, 8, 10, 12, 14, 16 are out-jogged inwards. You now pull the two packets apart, place the *inward* out-jogged cards in order face-down on the table and show the *outward* out-jogged cards to the two spectators, keeping them in order. Each spectator is asked to say if they see their mentally selected card. The two packets are then put together on the following basis: if both spectators answer "yes" or both answer "no" the hand they have looked at goes face-down on top of the other hand; if one has answered "yes" and the other has answered "no" then the hand they have *not* looked at goes on top of the hand they have looked at. This whole procedure is repeated two more times. You then perform one more "reverse faro", giving the *outward* out-jogged cards face-down to the first spectator and the *inward* out-jogged cards to the second spectator. When the spectators spell out their thought-of cards, using the spelling system described in the instructions for the trick *"Think of A Card – Spell Another"* they will arrive at each other's card. My first amendment to the presentation of the trick was to move to a pre-arrangement of the cards that would allow for dealing the cards out to the spectators rather than handing them out in a block. My second was to deal out the cards in an apparently random order as directed by the spectators. I also, at the same time, expanded the pre-arrangement to allow the cards to be dealt out into four hands – any one of which could be paired with any other. My next concern with the opening section of the trick was the fact that the spectators' choice of card was restricted to the middle six cards of a hand of eight cards. The first and last cards of the hands are there not to be spelled out but as an essential element in the mechanism of the locating and spelling process, whereas the middle six cards of each hand form a spelling-out sequence running from ten to fifteen letters. It occurred to me, however, that if the first and last card of each hand could be spelled out in nine letters and sixteen letters respectively then they too could be spelled out in the spelling-out process. Two problems arise in attempting to produce this outcome: the first is that there are no cards with nine or sixteen letters that spell out in the way used in the trick, and the second is that even if there were such cards the mechanics of the trick would require two cards of nine letters and two cards of sixteen letters. To simplify matters, the solution to both problems was to introduce identical *"Joker Card"*'s (nine letters) and *"The Invisible Card"*'s (sixteen letters) into all the hands. My next concerns were with the strange and suspicious handling of the cards involved in the series of four "reverse faros", and the fact that both spectators were directed to look for their cards in the same hand. What seemed to me much more natural and less suspicious was to order the cards in such a way that they could be dealt to the spectators who could then look for their card in the hand that had been dealt to them. The mechanics of the deals set out in the description of the trick *"Think of A Card – Spell*

Another" allow this to be done, the deals actually ordering the cards as necessary. All that was then required was to reverse the formula given by Fulves to allow for the search for the thought-of cards to be made in both hands. Finally, if the performer used a bridged card and a sequence of false cuts and shuffles the ordering of the cards could be made to appear totally random.

"Shuffle-Spell"

Jean Hugard describes the trick *"The Shuffled Spelling Bee"* in his book *Encyclopaedia of Card Tricks* (page 57 Dover edition; page 79 Foulsham edition). It relies for its effect on the pre-arrangement of the two black suits of the pack (Clubs: 2, K, 10, Q, 7, 3, 4, 9, 5, A, 6, 8, J; Spades: 3, 8, 7, A, Q, 6, 4, 2, J, K, 10, 9, 5). The red cards of the pack are mixed in any order. The Club cards are then placed on top of the red cards and the Spades beneath the red cards. Finally, a Joker card is placed at the middle of the red cards. With the pack so arranged it is possible using a sequence of riffle shuffles, and by extracting the Joker before one of the shuffles, to produce a pack in which the two pre-arranged suits, although distributed throughout the pack, will remain in the same pre-arranged order, allowing them to be extracted in the order shown above. This order allows the cards turned over from the top of the face-down Spades packet to be spelled out from the Clubs packet using the spelling system described for the trick *"Shuffle Spell"*. My version of the trick provides a stack and handling that brings all four suits into play. Again the use of a bridged card and false shuffles and false cuts at appropriate occasions during the performance would reinforce the impression that the cards were being indiscriminately mixed. If there is a weakness in my version of the trick it is that the open spread of the cards could allow a particularly observant spectator to see the pattern of cards in the sequences, but, given a quick spread, and the fact that the two sequences are mixed in reverse order, the chances of this happening are very small. In addition, the dealing and separating out of the cards would appear to unscramble any sequences.

"MIRASKILL DENIED"

Karl Fulves in his book *More Self-Working Card Tricks* (page 7) attributes the invention of the trick "Miraskil" (*sic*) to Stewart James and sets out a version of it developed by himself and Joseph K. Schmidt. There are many other versions. For example, Martin Gardner in his *Mathematics, Magic, and Mystery* (page 13) describes what he calls the *"Stewart James Colour Prediction"*, involving the secret removal of four cards from a full pack of cards to achieve its effect. Arthur F. MacTier in his book *Card Concepts* (pages 268/74) devotes a whole chapter to the principle involved and a variety of effects employing it, and Jean Hugard in his book *The Encyclopedia of Card Tricks* (pages 330/1 Dover edition; pages 373/4 Foulsham edition) also describes the trick, again involving the removal of four cards from the pack. In brief, the effect depends on the fact that if you take a pack or a packet of cards, shuffle it, and deal out the cards in pairs, then the like pairs (Red/Red or Black/Black) will be equal in number, or there will be no like pairs at all (although the probability of the latter occurring with a full pack is very low indeed). If you then take the same pack or packet and remove two cards of any one colour, shuffle the pack or packet, and deal out again, the deal will produce one more pair of the opposite colour to the cards you have taken out or a single pair of the colour you have not taken out (although again there is a very low probability with a full pack of producing no like pairs at all). My first intention was to develop the effect without the secret removal of cards from the pack. This was very easily achieved by dividing the pack into two equal packets and, after allowing a spectator a free choice of either of the two packets, inventing a subterfuge to allow the performer to count the cards of one colour in the other packet and thus be in a position to predict the difference in number in the pairs dealt out by the spectator from the other packet, or to predict that there would be an equal number of like pairs. However, I was not happy with either the presentation or the strength of the outcome. I then had the idea of using the discarded unlike pairs in some way to reverse the outcome of the dealing, ie. to deal out the whole pack, after it had been mixed and shuffled, without producing a single like pair – an almost impossible chance. To achieve this I turned to what is known as the Gilbreath stack. This is a pre-arrangement of the pack into a complete alternating colour sequence: Red-Black-Red-Black or Black-Red-Black-Red, etc. The stack is so named from Norman Gilbreath who observed that "if a (pack) of cards in the order of alternating cards is cut into two parts, with the bottom colours of the two parts (being) of opposite colours, and, the two parts are riffle shuffled together, then each successive pair of cards is composed of one red card and one black card" (quoted in Arthur F. MacTier's *Card Concepts* (page 160)). Obviously, if I could demonstrate to the spectator the almost certain probability of producing like pairs from a full pack and even a part pack and at the same time arrange to produce a Gilbreath stack in the discard pile, then if I took the discard pile and, after shuffling and mixing it, I produced not a single like pair in the dealing out, I had what I considered an impressive effect – thus *"Miraskill Denied"*.

"Can You Believe It?"

In the early 1940s Paul Curry developed an effect known as *"Out of This World"* which had as its outcome the separating out from a mixed face-down pack of all the red cards into one packet and all the black cards into another. In his book *Self-Working Close-up Card Magic* Karl Fulves describes it as "a modern-day classic" (page 114) and sets out the workings of a trick producing the effect using a pre-arrangement of the pack, two mugs into which the cards are placed as their face-colour is guessed at by a spectator, and four labelled cardboard markers to order the cards in the mugs according to the guesses made by the spectator. The pre-arrangement consists of the 26 red cards of the pack being placed on top of the 26 black cards with some form of secret marking on the back of the card in 26th position to indicate the division of the colours and to facilitate the cutting of the pack at this point. Two of the cardboard markers (A and B) are labelled with the same colour on both sides (ie. A: Red/Red; B: Black/Black) while the other two markers (C and D) are labelled with one colour on one side and the other colour on the other side (ie. Red/Black). The trick begins with the marker A being placed in one mug and the marker C (with the opposite colour label to A towards the spectators) being placed in the other mug. A spectator is then invited to guess the colour of each face-down card as it is taken from the top of the face-down pack. The cards are placed (unseen) in front of the appropriately labelled marker (they are, of course, all red-faced cards). When the performer reaches the secret mark indicating the separation of the colours her or she invites a second spectator to guess the face colour of the remaining cards and, to separate that spectator's cards from the first spectator's cards, the performer places the cardboard marker D in the mug containing marker

C with the label of marker D that faces the spectators showing the opposite colour to marker C. Marker D is placed in front of the cards already in the mug. Marker B is placed in the same way in the mug containing marker A. The performer then distributes the second spectator's cards into the mugs as appropriate, placing them in front of the markers (again unseen, but they are, of course, all black-faced cards). If the cards in the mug containing markers A and B are taken out, whichever way they are examined the sequences of red and black cards will correspond with the markers. The cards in the other mug are taken by the performer who spreads them face-up to show that they too correspond with the markers. To my mind there were two major weaknesses in this presentation. The first was that, although the two separate halves of the pack could be shuffled and cut, it was not possible at any point during the performance of the tricks to display the cards face-up. The second was that for the trick to succeed the fact that the markers C and D had different colour labels back and front needed to be concealed both during and at the conclusion of the performance of the trick. Fulves suggests means to overcome these weaknesses, but weaknesses they remain nevertheless. Fortunately, Arthur F. MacTier in his book *Card Concepts* (pages 268/74) approaches the presentation of the effect in an entirely different way, using a Gilbreath stack as described in the previous section of this chapter on *"Miraskill Denied"*. As it was possible to finish that trick with the cards in a Gilbreath stack I was attracted to MacTier's method of using such a stack as the basis of an *"Out of This World"* effect. I therefore drew heavily on his presentation in the method of separating the cards, but the trick, to my mind, is strengthened by the handling and particularly by the revelation of the two selected cards out of place in the two colour sequences.

"Prime Cut Selection"

The trick is essentially a bottom card force, using what Arthur F. MacTier in his *Card Concepts* (page 55) refers to as the *"George Sands' Prime Number Principle"*. In the context of the trick *"Prime Cut Selection"* the principle could be summarised as that if you take a face-down packet of cards in which the total number of cards is a prime number and transfer from the top of the packet to the bottom a number of cards between 1 and the total number of cards in the packet, transferring the cards singly and turning over (ie. face-up) the last card being transferred, and if you repeat this procedure, using the same number, until only one card in the packet remains face-down, then that face-down card will be what was the bottom card of the packet. MacTier in discussing the principle and describing an effect using it gives credit to Peter Duffie for the development of a trick on which his own is based. This is performed with the cards face-up and involves the prediction by the performer of the card that will be left face-up at the conclusion of the trick. My version of the force and of the trick allows the cards to be used face-down and uses a card selected by a spectator as the revealed card.

"Divination"

Jean Hugard and Frederick Braué in *The Royal Road to Card Magic* (pages 136-8) describe a trick to which they give the title *"An Incomprehensible Divination"*. They refer to it as an "old war horse". The effect is based on placing Ace to 10 in that order as the top of a packet with a Joker card at the bottom of the packet. The packet is then given a Charlier Shuffle with the performer secretly sighting the top card of the packet after the shuffle. The value of this card (with the Joker card counting as 11) is used to provide the performer with a key number. This the performer produces by subtracting the value of the top card from 12. The performer then invites the spectator to think of any number between 1 and 10 and secretly to transfer one by one that number of cards from the top to the bottom of the packet. The performer takes the packet and cuts the card at his key number to the top of the packet. He or she then asks the spectator to state the number of cards moved and when the top card of the packet is turned over its value is this number. This card is turned face-down on the top of the packet giving the performer the means to calculate a new key number and to continue the trick. For this second phase of the trick the performer names a number (which is the key number) and invites the spectator to think of any number between 1 and 10 and again secretly to make the appropriate transfer of cards from the top to the bottom of the packet. When the performer makes the necessary transfer of cards the card at the top of the packet will be of the value of the number thought of by the spectator. Again, turning the card face-down on the top of the packet provides the performer with the means of calculating yet another key number and the trick may be continued. The Joker is provided in the stack in the event of any spectator attempting to subvert the trick by not moving any cards. In that case when the performer's cut is completed then the top card of the pack will be the Joker card. This is an excellent trick, but I felt that a totally different and equally strong effect could be achieved using the same principle. My idea was to use two sequences of Ace to King in place of the Ace to 10 and Joker card sequence used by Hugard and Braué. The first advantage of such an arrangement was that the card to be sighted to arrive at the key number could be the bottom card of the packet, and the second advantage was that if a card of any value was added to the key number then the card arrived at that position in the packet would be equal in value to the card value added. I could therefore give the other 26 cards of the pack to the spectator and allow him or her to choose any card from those 26 and, by adding the value of that card to my key number, match his card with a card of the same value from my packet without any transfer of cards from top to bottom, ie. I could deal out cards from the top of my packet or count the cards off the top of the packet. Finally, if I declared my number by choosing an appropriately valued card from the spectator's packet before he or she chose the card then the effect would be even stronger. All that was required then was to conceal the ordering of my packet and the mechanism of the trick and this I decided could be effectively achieved by either false cuts or false shuffles and/or a riffle shuffle and/or the use of a bridged card.

"CERTAIN CARD SNAP"

The development of this trick proceeded in such a strange way that it is worth describing at length. The initial inspiration was *"The Certain Card Trick"* developed by Percy Abbott and described by Jean Hugard and Frederick Braué in their *Expert Card Techniques* (pages 404/5). In studying the trick as they described it I had a number of reservations about its presentation. The original trick required that the pack be reduced to 48 cards to allow for the subsequent lay-out of the cards. It also required that the performer knew the identity of the bottom card in this 48 card packet. The spectator is asked to cut the packet and note the face-card at the bottom of the cut. As he or she does so the performer estimates the number of cards that the spectator cut-off. Then begins what I felt was a very complicated method of identifying the noted card. You begin by dividing your estimate of the number of cards taken by 6. This will give you a number, or a number plus a remainder. You ignore the remainder and take the number as your key number. The specator is now instructed to cut the pack and then to deal out (face-up) from the packet, which has been re-constituted by placing the cut-off cards back onto the top of the packet, six cards side by side, then another six cards below them, and so on until there are six rows of cards with each row containing eight cards. The spectator then declares in which row he or she sees the noted card and the performer can then secretly calculate the position in the row of the noted card using the following formula: Add your key number to the number of cards down the row in which you see your known card (ie. what was the bottom card of the packet): if the spectator has indicated that his noted card is in the same row as your noted card then it is in a position in that row equal to your calculation plus 1 (if the number is over 8 subtract 8): if the spectator has indicated a row to the right (from your point of view) of the row with your known card in it the noted card is in the same position down in that row as your calculation (again if it is over 8 subtract 8): if the spectator has indicated a row to the left of your known card then the noted card is at a position in that row equal to your calculation plus 1 (again if this number is over 8 subtract 8). My first thought was to simplify the formula for locating the noted card, and my second was to devise a means of allowing the cards to be placed face-down. Hugard and Braué in their version had suggested that a face-down lay-out of the cards could be achieved by marking the known card in some way so it was a simple matter for me to conclude that I could use a bridged card in place of such a marked card. It also occurred to me that if my bridged card was at the bottom of the pack as dealt then the bridged card would always be the last card dealt, that the noted card would always be to its left or in the same row, and that the position of the noted card in its row would always be equal to the key number. I thus had my simplified formula and the cards could be dealt out face-down. I also noted that if my known card (ie. the bridged card) was in a fixed position (which it was) then the noted card was always in the same position in whichever row it was. Two possibilities arose from this. The first was that if I could restrict the spectator's choice of cards to six possible cards I could predict without any calculation the position in the row of any of those cards. The second was that it did not matter in what order those cards were placed they would still finish in that same position in one of the rows. After a number of trials exploring these possibilities it became clear that the ideal spread for the selection of cards was eight cards and that to guarantee a cut into these cards half the packet should be used. Then by dealing the reconstituted packet out into eight 6-card rows I could be sure that the noted card was at the second position down in whatever row it was – and the dealing out of the cards in six card sequences could deliver any card of that sequence to any row. I also noted that if the bottom half of the packet was used then the card noted in that half would be dealt out as the next to last card in whatever row it was dealt to, ie. the card noted in the top half would be one down from the top of the row it was dealt to and the card noted in the bottom half would be one up from the bottom of its row. Thus if one half was reversed in order a game of "Snap" would bring both cards together. This led me to the conclusion that I could involve two spectators, each choosing a card from a 24-card packet. After a number of trials along these lines I decided that I could guarantee a selection from the middle eight cards of a 24-card packet by dealing out six 8-card hands and allowing the spectators to choose any card in any hand. This also meant that I could allow the spectators to shuffle all the hands both before and after selection. All this, of course, was taking me further and further away from Abbott's original trick, but I felt that the outcome was equally, if not more, mystifying and striking.

"Just Think of An Ace"

The trick depends for its effect on the fortunate fact that the number of letters in spelling out the Aces can be manipulated to produce a sequence: AC (10), AH (11), AD (13). Thus any one of them could be spelled out by taking the card placed at the appropriate position in the pack. AS (11) can be accommodated into the sequence by placing it between AH (11) and AD (13) and by taking the card left on top of the packet, ie. the 12th card. The essence of the trick therefore becomes the handling and manipulation required to position the Aces.

"A Magic Number"

In his *Mathematics, Magic, and Mystery* (pages 7/8) Martin Gardner describes a trick with the title *"A Baffling Prediction"* in which a spectator chooses four cards from any twelve cards from the pack. The eight cards not chosen are returned to the bottom of the pack. The performer then takes each of the chosen cards in turn and deals out onto each card the number of cards required to bring the total to 10 (ie. on a 3 the performer would deal seven cards), the picture or court cards counting as 10s receive no cards. The spectator now totals the values of the original four cards he or she chose and counts down the remainder of the pack to the card at this number which will be what was the bottom card of the pack at the very start of the trick and which the performer could therefore have predicted. Gardner follows this with a description of the improvement made to this trick by Henry Christ which takes it to a different level. In this version the spectator selects any card from any nine cards from the pack. He or she places the selected card on top of the cards not selected and the remainder of the pack on top of this packet. The trick then proceeds as I have described for the trick *"A Magic Number"*. My own version uses eight cards from the pack from which the spectator may select his or her card. This is to allow for the use of the bridged card, and the use of false cuts and false shuffles to obscure the ordering of the pack. Obviously, the "secret" of the trick is the positioning of the selected card as the 9th card from the bottom of the pack. The mathematical principle involved is illustrated below:

BASIC TRICK

Value of First Card	3 6 8 2 = 19			
No. of Cards Placed	7 4 2 8			
Total No. of Cards Used	8 5 3 9 = 25			
52 − 25 = 27 − 19 = 8				
Value of First Card	8	K(10)	2	A	= 21
No. of Cards Placed	2	−	8	9	
Total No. of Cards Used	3	1	9	10	= 23
52 − 23 = 29 − 21 = 8					

HENRY CHRIST'S VARIATION

Value of Coincident Card	2	5	–		6 = 13
No. of Cards Placed	9	6		11	5 = 31
52 – 31 = 21 – 13 = 8					
Value of Coincident Card	6 8 2 1 = 17				
No. of Cards Placed	5 3 9 10 = 27				
52 – 27 = 25 – 17 = 8					

"REAL MAGIC"

This trick developed from studying the trick *"The Magic of Manhattan"* described by Martin Gardner in his *Mathematics, Magic, and Mystery* (pages 20/1). In that trick the cards are cut near the centre of the pack by a spectator, who then takes either packet, counts the cards in it, and notes the card at the position from the bottom of the packet which is indicated by adding together the digits of the number of cards in the packet. The spectator then places the packet on top of the other packet to reconstitute the pack. Using this procedure the noted card will always be at the 19th position from the top of the pack so that if the performer then spells out the phrase *"The Magic of Manhattan"* or any other nineteen letter phrase he or she will arrive at the noted card. It occurred to me that the effect could be strengthened by allowing the spectator to cut off any number of cards above 10 and then by adjusting the order of the cut-off cards and controlling their position in the re-constituted pack it would be possible, using one of four suitable phrases, to arrive at the noted card. This version also allows all the counting, including that by the spectator, to be done from the top of the pack and the packet, which is a much more natural procedure than counting up from the bottom of the packet as in the original trick.

"NOBODY KNOWS ANYTHING"

The effect is achieved by an adaptation of the *"Shuffle-Bored"* principle developed by Simon Aronson (*Bound to Please*, pages 145-71) and also discussed by Arthur F. MacTier in his *Card Concepts* (pages 100-06). In essence the principle is that if a pack of cards is divided into two packets and if a number of cards from each packet are turned over and shuffled into the other packet and this process is repeated as many times as wished, then, if, finally, one of the packets is turned over and shuffled into the other packet, the pack will contain the original two packets, one face-up and the other face-down. Some years earlier Bob Hummer had noted a very similar effect based on the fact that if a face-down packet containing an even number of cards was taken and the top two cards were turned face-up and the pack then cut and completed, and this process was repeated as many times as wished then if every other card in the packet was turned over the number of face-up cards in the packet would be half the total number of cards in the packet (see MacTier's *Card Concepts*, page 107 and Gardner's *Mathematics, Magic, and Mystery*, pages 17/19). For the trick *"Nobody Knows Anything"* I have used two packs of cards and a sequence of riffle shuffles to add to the "confusion". The use of the bridged card allows the division of the pack for these shuffles to be controlled.

"SAME NUMBER – SAME CARD"

In his book *Card Concepts* (pages 34/36) Arthur F. MacTier sets out and discusses two "principles" involving counting sequences using packs of cards. The first was developed by Martin D. Kruskel and the second came from an effect developed by Alexander F. Kraus. The former is based on the fact that if you take a pack of cards and turn over the first card at the top of the pack and then go to the card at the position in the pack indicated by the value of the first card and turn that card over, take the value of that card as a new starting point and go through the pack repeating this process, you will eventually arrive at the last card in the pack or at a card with a value greater than the number of the cards left in the pack. If this card is noted and the whole process is repeated, again and again, using the second card of the pack as the starting point, then the third, then the fourth, etc. there is a fair probability that you will finish the sequence on the same card. In fact, the probability is the probability of the sequencing coinciding at some point. This probability can be significantly increased by a number of subterfuges, eg. by counting the picture or court cards as 10s, or, even better, as 1s. MacTier then describes a very elegant and striking effect using this principle. It uses two packs of cards. In essence the trick consists of the spectator and the performer each thinking of a number from 1 to 10 and using that number as the starting point of the process described above for their own pack. The packs are then exchanged, the order of the packs not being disturbed. The spectator and the performer then go through the counting process again, this time using their own thought-of number as the starting point. Each should arrive at the other's card. Although the probability of success is quite high it is still only a probability, and MacTier considers it prudent to provide a means of disguising failure. However, the second principle can have a guaranteed outcome in that if a sequence of cards from King through to Ace is placed on the bottom of a pack and if a card is taken from near the top of the pack and used as the first card in the counting process then the total of the turned-up cards will always be 52. Moreover, the cards above the stack may be shuffled on each count and there is no requirement to adjust the values of the high value cards thus they can be given their actual values: J (11), Q (12), K (13). It occurred to me that the two "principles" could be combined to use the guaranteed outcome of the second "principle" to disguise the fact that the first "principle" had not led to a successful outcome. In fact, given that the totalling effect would work every time, there was a fair probability that the "each participant finds the other's card" would work and a very fair probability that one of the cards would be arrived at in the counting-out process. However, there are further variations of the second "principle" from which it is possible to develop other effects with a guaranteed outcome. The first variation I tried was of retaining the King to Ace stack at the bottom of the pack and cutting a number of cards from the top of the pack. Thus, when you have completed the counting out process described above the number of cards cut off would be equal to 52 minus the total arrived at by the counting process. For example, if you could secretly remove say five cards from the pack before the counting out began then you could predict that the total arrived at would be 47 (52 − 5). Alternatively, you could allow a spectator to select the starting point in the pack for the count (say, the 5th card down) and predict that the total arrived at would be 48 (52 − 5 = 47 + 1 = 48). If the selected starting point was the 15th card in the pack then the total arrived at would be 38 (52 − 15 = 37 plus 1 = 38). The second variation I tried was to place a King through Ace stack at the top of the pack and a King through Ace stack at the bottom of the pack. With this pre-arrangement it would be possible to predict that the total arrived at by the counting process would be 52 minus the selected number plus 1. You could also, if the count was repeated without disturbing the order of the pack, but with a different starting point, predict that the total arrived at would be 52 minus the second selected number plus 1, and that at the end of the second count you would arrive at the same card as on the first count. In fact, the second card in the counting process will always begin the same sequence irrespective of what number is selected as the starting point, ie. it will be the 14th card from the top of the pack. The third variation of this second "principle" arises from the observation that it can be applied to a packet of cards as well as to the whole pack. For example, if you remove from the pack the picture or court cards you will be left with a packet of 40 cards. If you then place a 10 through to Ace at the bottom of this packet and ask a spectator at what number card in the packet he or she wishes to begin the counting process, the total that will be arrived at will be 40 minus the number selected plus 1. If you repeat the process for another number, without disturbing the order of the packet, you will arrive at a different total number but one that you could have predicted immediately the spectator had chosen at what point in the packet he or she wished the counting process to start. All these variations had the potential to produce a strong effect but obviously there were many more variations hidden away behind the principle which had equal potential. I determined to try to find some of them. After much experimentation I came to a number of conclusions. The first was that the stack at the top of the pack could be eliminated either by using a thought-of number or by using a card to which the spectator could assign any value. My second conclusion was that in the counting processes leading to an over-all total I could allow the spectator to choose any card in the packets counted out without affecting the eventual outcome of the total number: it was only when I wished to arrive at the same card in two counts that the cards needed to be kept in the same order within the packets. The third conclusion arose out of the need to disguise the placing of the stack at the bottom of the pack and I concluded that this could be achieved by misdirecting the attention of the spectator by asking him or her to sort though the cards in the pack extracting certain cards and that the most logical cards for the spectator to be searching for were the picture or court cards. This line of thought re-inforced my next conclusion that a number of cards less than the full pack produced a less suspicion-inducing total than the 52 produced by the full pack. It also reduced the stack from thirteen down to a more manageable ten cards. However, my most startling conclusion was that if the 10 to Ace sequence was placed *within* the pack then not only did it guarantee that the dealing would finish on the same card but it also guaranteed that the total arrived at would (if the order of the cards was not disturbed) always be the same irrespective of the starting number. A few moments thought shows why. After entry into the 10 to Ace sequence the subsequent cards will always be the same and thus have the same total number. The cards preceding the 10 to Ace sequence plus the card arrived at in the sequence will also have the same total number. Thus the two separate totals added together will always give the same overall total. It was out of these thoughts and conclusions that I eventually arrived at the trick *"Same Number—Same Card"*.

"Everybody Shouts"

This is a classic effect in card magic. It has been described and performed in many variations. In its basic form it is the forcing of the same card on a number of spectators and then revealing that card in a striking way to all of the spectators at the same time. It is usually known as *"Everybody's Card"*. Hugard and Braué describe a version of the trick suitable for performance before a theatre-sized audience involving two forces, and four sleights-of-hand to change the top card of the pack. Mercifully, they also describe the trick adapted for performance before a smaller audience that reduces the requirement for manipulation – but not by much (*The Royal Road to Card Magic*, pages 281/7). However, in his *Encyclopaedia of Card Tricks* (page 97 Dover Edition: page 109 Foulsham edition) Hugard reduces the handling requirement to forcing only, using what is known as a "slick" card, which is a card highly polished on its face so that it can be easily located in the pack. It is this version I have taken as the basis for *"Everybody Shouts"*, using the bridged card in place of the "slick" card. The use of the bridged card in this way enables the performer to allow the spectators to do what they will with the pack in the way of shuffles and cuts after they have placed the selected card back into the pack. There is a weakness in the requirement for each spectator to take either the top or bottom card of the pack as the selected card. This could be overcome by varying the forcing method used. However, my own preference is to keep the process as simple as possible. It is safer and still convincing to perform the trick as described in the chapter on *"The Final Tricks"*.

Arranging a Stack for Spelling or Dealing

There are a number of tricks described in this book that require the pre-arrangement of the pack or packet to allow the cards to be spelled out. Others require the placing of a pre-ordered stack in the pack, arranged in such a way that it can be dealt out. On the assumption that it might be of interest and use to the reader some methods that can be used to do this are described in this section.

SPELLING ARRANGEMENTS

Hugard in his *Encyclopaedia of Card Tricks* (page 41, Dover edition: page 61, Foulsham edition) describes a method of arranging a packet of cards in such a way that the cards from Ace through to King can be spelled out by taking a card in turn for each letter of the spelling from the top of the face-down packet, transferring these cards face-down in turn to the bottom of the packet and turning over the card then at the top of the packet to reveal the spelled-out card. This card is then removed from the packet and placed on the table. The procedure begins by marking out on a sheet of paper thirteen spaces and then moving along the spaces from left to right spelling out the letters of A – C – E. You then enter A in the next space and continue on from the space after the one you have filled, spelling out T – W – O and entering 2 in the next space. You continue in this way, always moving from left to right and skipping over any occupied space, until you have filled all the spaces. You will find that at the end of the process you will finish with an order of cards 3 – 8 – 7 – A – Q – 6 – 4 – 2 – J – K – 10 – 9 – 5 and you will find that from this order you are able to spell out all the cards from Ace to King using the spelling system described above.

The system can be adapted to spell out any sequence. For example, to spell out 4, 8, 3, and King in that order from a 9-card packet begin by marking out the nine spaces. After spelling out F – O – U – R place the figure 4 in the next space. If you then go to the next space and spell out E – I – G – H – T you will place the figure 8 in the 2nd space, and, following the same procedure, you will spell out T – H – R – E – E and place the figure 3 in the last space, and after spelling out K – I – N – G you will place the letter K in the 7th space. The stack you require therefore is X – 8 – X – X – 4 – X – K – X – 3 (where X is any card).

An alternative method of achieving the same end using the cards themselves to determine the necessary ordering can be used. To do this begin by taking a sequence of cards from Ace through to King and placing them face-up on the table with Ace at the left end of the row and King at the right end of the row. Now spell out A – C – E beginning at the left end of the row and moving along the cards counting a letter on each card. When you have reached the end, pick up the card immediately to its right (which will be the 4), take the Ace from its position at the beginning of the row and place it face-down at the position vacated by the 4. Now place the 4 face-up at the position vacated by the Ace. Starting with the first face-up card after the face-down Ace count out T – W – O, pick up the next card (which will be the 8), take the 2 from its position and place it face-down at the position vacated by the 8 and place the 8 face-up in the position vacated by the 2. Now, starting with the first face-up card after the face-down 2 spell out T – H – R – E – E, counting along the row. This will bring you to the end of the row so the first face-up card is at the beginning of the row (it is, of course, the 4). Pick up the 4, take the 3 from its position and place it face-down at the position vacated by the 4 and place the 4 face-up at the position vacated by the 3. Now, starting with the first face-up card after the face-down 3, spell and count out F – O – U – R (ignoring any face-down card in the counting out), take the next face-up card (which will be the 7) and transpose it with the 4, placing the 7 face-up and the 4 face-down. Continue with this spelling and counting and, when necessary, transposing procedure, ingnoring any face-down cards, until all the cards but the King are face-down. (You will find that the final positions of the 6, 7 and 8 do not require any transposition). If you then turn the cards face-up along the row you will see that you have arrived at the arrangement required.

DEALING ARRANGEMENTS

For the purpose of illustration a worst case scenario will be assumed and that is that you wish to deal out face-down from a face-down pack two 26-card piles which, after they have been examined, will have the second pile placed on top of the first. You then wish to deal out from the re-constituted pack four 13-card hands, each in a particular order, ie. Hearts, Clubs, Diamonds, Spades in that order, each with Ace to King with Ace as the top card of each face down hand. All deals to be consecutive dealing, ie. a card in turn to each hand or pile. The following tables are the basis on which the required organisation of the cards can be determined.

HANDS REQUIRED

Hand 1: (Top):	1 – 2 – 3 – 4 – 5 – 6 – 7 – 8 – 9 – 10 – 11 – 12 – 13
Hand 2: (Top):	14 – 15 – 16 – 17 – 18 – 19 – 20 – 21 – 22 – 23 – 24 – 25 – 26
Hand 3: (Top):	27 – 28 – 29 – 30 – 31 – 32 – 33 – 34 – 35 – 36 – 37 – 38 – 39
Hand 4: (Top):	40 – 41 – 42 – 43 – 44 – 45 – 46 – 47 – 48 – 49 – 50 – 51 – 52

PACK REQUIRED FOR DEALING (FACE-DOWN)

(Top):	13 – 26 – 39 – 52 // 12 – 25 – 38 – 51 // 11 – 24 – 37 – 50 // 10 – 23 – 36 – 49 // 9 – 22 – 35 – 48 // 8 – 21 – 34 – 47 // 7 – 20 – **33** – **46** // **6** – **19** – **32** – **45** // **5** – **18** – **31** – **44** // **4** – **17** – **30** – **43** // **3** – **16** – **29** – **42** // **2** – **15** – **28** – **41** // **1** – **14** – **27** – **40**

REQUIRED TWO PILE DEAL (FACE-DOWN)

(Pile B to be placed on Pile A to re-constitute pack)

Hand A: (Top):	33 – 46 – 6 – 19 – 32 – 45 – 5 – 18 – 31 – 44 – 4 – 17 – 30 – 43 – 3 – 16 – 29 – 42 – 2 – 15 – 28 – 41 – 1 – 14 – 27 – 40
Hand B: (Top):	13 – 26 – 39 – 52 – 12 – 25 – 38 – 51 – 11 – 24 – 37 – 50 – 10 – 23 – 36 – 49 – 9 – 22 – 35 – 48 – 8 – 21 – 34 – 47 – 7 – 20

PACK REQUIRED TO DEAL TWO PILES (FACE-DOWN)

(Top):	40 – 20 – 27 – 7 – 14 – 47 – 1 – 34 – 41
	21 – 28 – 8 – 15 – 48 – 2 – 35 – 42
	22 – 29 – 9 – 16 – 49 – 3 – 36 – 43
	23 – 30 – 10 – 17 – 50 – 4 – 37 – 44
	24 – 31 – 11 – 18 – 51 – 5 – 38 – 45
	25 – 32 – 12 – 19 – 52 – 6 – 39 – 46
	26 – 33 – 13

APPLIED TO FOUR-HAND DEAL TO GIVE ACE TO KING SEQUENCE IN HEARTS, CLUBS, DIAMONDS, SPADES IN THAT ORDER, THROUGH A TWO PILE DEAL

1	2	3	4	5	6	7	8	9	10	11	12	13
AH	2H	3H	4H	5H	6H	7H	8H	9H	10H	JH	QH	KH

14	15	16	17	18	19	20	21	22	23	24	25	26
AC	2C	3C	4C	5C	6C	7C	8C	9C	10C	JC	QC	KC

27	28	29	30	31	32	33	34	35	36	37	38	39
AD	2D	3D	4D	5D	6D	7D	8D	9D	10D	JD	QD	KD

40	41	42	43	44	45	46	47	48	49	50	51	52
AS	2S	3S	4S	5S	6S	7S	8S	9S	10S	JS	QS	KS

REQUIRED PACK (FACE-DOWN)

(Top):	AS	—	7C	—	AD	—	7H	—	AC	—	8S	—	AH	—	8D
—	2S	—	8C	—	2D	—	8H	—	2C	—	9S	—	2H	—	9D
—	3S	—	9C	—	3D	—	9H	—	3C	—	10S	—	3H	—	10D
—	4S	—	10C	—	4D	—	10H	—	4C	—	JS	—	4H	—	JD
—	5S	—	JC	—	5D	—	JH	—	5C	—	QS	—	5H	—	QD
—	6S	—	QC	—	6D	—	QH	—	6C	—	KS	—	6H	—	KD
—	7S	—	KC	—	7D	—	KH								

The example illustrates the process. Any required hands can be produced by substituting the identities of the required cards as appropriate and by adjusting the numbers in the tables to correspond with the number of cards in use.